Seven Principles of

DOING LIVE THERAPY
DEMONSTRATIONS

By the same author

When Time Is at a Premium: Cognitive-Behavioural Approaches to Single-Session Therapy and Very Brief Coaching (2016)

Attitudes in Rational Emotive Behaviour Therapy (REBT): Components, Characteristics and Adversity-Related Consequences (2016)

'Seven Principles' Series

Seven Principles of Good Mental Health (2021)

Seven Principles of Rational Emotive Behaviour Therapy (2021)

Seven Principles of Single-Session Therapy (2021)

Seven Principles of the Working Alliance in Therapy (2022)

Seven Principles of

DOING LIVE THERAPY DEMONSTRATIONS

Windy Dryden, PhD

Rationality Publications

Rationality Publications
136 Montagu Mansions, London W1U 6LQ

www.rationalitypublications.com
info@rationalitypublications.com

First edition published by Rationality Publications
Copyright (c) 2021 Windy Dryden

A catalogue record of this book is
available from the British Library.

First edition 2021

ISBN: 978-1-910301-97-5

Contents

Introduction

I first trained as a counsellor in 1974–5 at the University of Aston in Birmingham. The course was rooted in client-centred therapy – the term 'person centred therapy' had not yet been created – and we studied client-centred theory and how it impacted the practice of counselling. However, it was only when I saw the film where Carl Rogers worked with Gloria that I realised how I was supposed to work with clients and decided that while I agreed with much of the theory of client-centred therapy I was not really suited to its practice.

Later in the course, we studied other approaches to counselling and saw Fritz Perls demonstrate Gestalt Therapy and Albert Ellis demonstrate Rational-Emotive Therapy (as it was known then[1]) both of whom worked with Gloria. Watching these films helped me to decide that my ideas about counselling and its practice were most in 'sync' with RET and after qualifying as a counsellor I undertook training in RET at what is now the Albert Ellis Institute in New York. While the therapy demonstration of RET carried out by Ellis with

---

[1] RET became Rational Emotive Behaviour Therapy (REBT) in 1993.

Gloria was not the finest example of RET (see Weinrach, 2001) I saw enough to conclude that this was a therapeutic approach with which I resonated.

I did not realise it at the time, but I what I learned was that watching demonstrations of therapy helped me learn more about psychotherapy and counselling than reading books on the subject and even than engaging in short role-plays. Later in my career as a therapy educator and trainer, I always incorporated live therapy demonstrations in my workshops and training courses. I did so because I realised that while talking about the theory and practice of therapy is important, it will only take you so far as a trainer. What really counts is to show people how ideas about theory and therapy can be implemented in real life therapeutic encounters.

Some trainers will demonstrate their way of working but only with volunteers who are asked to play the role of a client. They will not invite the person to discuss a real problem for which they would like to receive help. This has never been my practice. I think that it is important to do a therapy demonstration that is real for several reasons.

First, a therapy session where the person brings a current problem for which they would like help is a genuine encounter and echoes the importance of genuineness as a vital ingredient of effective therapy. When a person plays the role of a client, they either stick to the role too closely or they give it up too easily. The role-play therefore lacks an experiential basis. It is quite common for a demonstration of therapy to be done where the 'client' is an actor who has been trained to play the role of a client (see Hopwood, Swenson, Bateman, Yeomans & Gunderson, 2014). This is a valid approach when the welfare of the person would otherwise be threatened if they were to discuss a real problem. However, leaving this aside, what such a therapy demonstration cannot show is how a real person responds to therapy when they are working with their own personal material.

Second, doing a live therapy demonstration session in front of an audience requires the therapist to be brave – to show to what extent they practise what they preach. The therapist reveals how they work to an audience who may be critical of their efforts. They also have to be prepared to show how they work warts and all, including mistakes that they may make. I am willing to take these risks largely because while being a therapist is important to me, it does not define me as a person. Consequently, I am prepared to admit errors that I have made in the demonstrations of therapy that I give. I can do so because my worth as a person is not defined by my therapeutic prowess or lack thereof. I am also happy to receive critical comments from members of the audience and can do so because while such comments can be uncomfortable they help me to learn. Such matters are important because they show that even an experienced therapist makes errors and that it is no big deal to admit them. As such, I believe that I am being a good role model as a therapist. It is ironic, therefore, that while members of the audience watching a live therapy demonstration frequently comment that a volunteer that I have counselled has been brave for volunteering, I have never had anyone say that I have been brave in demonstrating how I work in a public professional setting.

The third reason why genuine live therapy demonstrations are better than role-played demonstrations is that the volunteer can give experiential feedback on how the session impacted them as a person. In my experience, the most common question that a volunteer is asked at the end of a therapy demonstration is 'How did it feel to have the session?' (see Principle 7). It is much easier for the person to answer this question if they have discussed a genuine current concern for which that have sought help than if they have role-played another person with a fictitious problem.

People sometimes say that live therapy demonstrations cheapen the nature of therapy which is, in essence, a private and confidential relationship. While it is the case that a live therapy demonstration is a public event, it is also the case that the audience is asked to assert that they will adhere to the principle of 'what is said here, stays here'. Also, both the therapist and the volunteer agree to have a therapeutic conversation that they both know will be observed. They are, thus, both, in effect, giving their informed consent to having the conversation in front of an audience.

Before I present a brief outline of the book, I want to make to make three points clear. First, I will only be discussing live demonstrations of therapy rather than those that have been pre-recorded, Second, I will only be referring to live demonstrations of entire therapy sessions no matter how long or short they last. Thus, I will not be discussing situations where a therapist demonstrates a particular skill only. Third, I will be discussing two different types of therapy demonstrations: demonstrations of single-session therapy (SST) and demonstrations of Rational Emotive Behaviour Therapy (REBT). While there is overlap between the two types of demonstrations, the emphasis is different. My REBT demonstrations feature the practice of Rational Emotive Behaviour Therapy but are informed by single-session thinking (see Dryden 2021a) and my SST demonstrations feature the practice of single-session therapy, but are informed by a number of therapeutic orientations, the main one being REBT (see Dryden 2021b). I will make it clear which type of demonstration session I am discussing where appropriate.

*

In this book, then, I will begin by discussing the multi-purposive nature of live therapy demonstrations and the role of the context in which these demonstrations occur. In the rest of the book, I will discuss my own work in conducting such live demonstrations. First, I will detail three frameworks that guide my work in live therapy demonstrations: (i) the working alliance; (ii) single session thinking; (iii) REBT's ABC framework. Then, I will show how to get a live therapy demonstration off to a good start, before emphasising the importance of focusing on and understanding the person's nominated problem in context. From there I will discuss how I look for ways of helping the person to bring about change in their nominated problem before, in the final chapter, showing the importance of ending well. In the book's appendices, I show the importance of practising what I preach and will present and comment on a transcript of a live therapy demonstration of SST and one of REBT that I have conducted.

Windy Dryden
London & Eastbourne
May 2021

PRINCIPLE 1

The Multi-Purposive Nature of Doing Live Therapy Demonstrations

In this opening principle, I will discuss the three main purposes of therapy demonstrations: educational, therapeutic and entertainment. While these purposes interact, I will deal with them separately.

The Educational Purpose of Live Therapy Demonstrations

There is a plethora of written material on psychotherapy. This material focuses on the theory that underpins the practice of psychotherapy and on the practice itself. However, while reading such material is vital to the acquisition of knowledge, it does not demonstrate how therapy is practised. The best way that this is done is by observing therapists practising therapy and preferably doing so live. This point is recognised in the education of other professionals. For example, when medical doctors learn how to perform surgery, they will observe skilled surgeons carrying out live operations before they are permitted to perform surgery themselves. If you need to have an operation, would you want the procedure you need to have to be carried out by someone who has never observed it being implemented by highly skilled surgeons? Of course, you wouldn't!

Thus, after learning about the practice of therapy in books and before seeing actual clients, it is important for therapists learning their craft to observe good examples of its practice and to be able to ask questions about what they have observed.

From an educational perspective, then, before seeing a live therapy demonstration, a person needs to understand what it is they are going to be seeing. They need a framework to help them understand what it is to be demonstrated and why this is deemed to be therapeutic. Thus, before watching a live therapy demonstration, in my view, a person needs to have a prior opportunity to be presented with material on the relevant therapeutic approach, ask questions about it and to voice any doubts, reservations and objections (DROs) that they may have to this material. Once the therapy trainer has answered their questions and responded to their DROs, the person is ready to watch live demonstrations of the therapeutic approach being learned.

My Preferred Practice

My own practice has always been to do demonstrations myself live with a volunteer from the attending audience. Alternatives to this practice are for me to show a video recording of a therapy demonstration that I have done in the past or a video of someone else doing a therapy demonstration.

The reasons for my preferred practice are as follows. First, there is a greater chance of consistency between the didactic part of the training and the therapy demonstration if I do them both than if I show someone else giving the demonstration. My live demonstration will illustrate my teaching better than a pre-recorded demonstration, since in the live demo, I will have the points that I made in the pre-demonstration lectures fresh in my mind. Second, the audience can ask the volunteer for their perspective on the session if the demonstration is live. If this happens, I can also dialogue with the volunteer on points that either of us have made during the 'question and answer' period that follows the live demonstration. In pre-recorded demonstrations either given by me or by someone else, the audience has no chance to ask the volunteer any questions because the volunteer is absent.

Finally, pre-recorded demonstrations are more likely to be selected because they are good examples of the therapy approach being taught with errors kept to a minimum. In a live therapy demonstration, by contrast, nobody knows, in advance, how it is going to turn out and, in this regard, it mirrors what happens in everyday clinical practice. When I make errors in live therapy demonstrations there is much to be gained by showing the audience these errors. They get to learn that errors are made by all therapists, both novice and experienced and because I am prepared to admit to making errors in a non-defensive manner then assuming such an attitude helps trainee therapists not be anxious about making their own errors when they have an opportunity to practise the relevant approach in peer counselling work.[2] Another advantage of making errors in live therapy demonstrations is that the audience can see that the volunteer can have a useful therapeutic conversation despite the errors that I have made.

I mentioned in the introduction that I decided to pursue training REBT after watching a demonstration that Albert Ellis did with Gloria. When people watch my live demonstrations of therapy, they can do two things, only the first of which I was able to do while watching the Ellis–Gloria demonstration. First, they can determine whether they resonate with the mode of practice being demonstrated and whether they want to

---

[2] Peer counselling is where two people take turns at assuming the role of a therapist helping the other person with their current, genuine concerns using the therapy approach that they have observed in the live therapy demonstrations.

pursue further training in the method. Second, they can ask me questions about what I did and why I did it, which can also help them make their decision. So, when I give a live therapy demonstration, I not only show what I did, I can also make explicit the thinking that informed my practice (see Dryden, 2009).

The Therapeutic Purpose of Live Therapy Demonstrations

People do not usually choose to have therapy in front of an audience as their first choice of how they would prefer to seek help. Such live therapeutic conversations occur in the context of therapy training workshops and other educational programmes and would probably not occur if these events were not taking place. Thus, although I have done over 500 live therapy demonstrations, I have never worked with a person who wanted help from me only if it were to be in front of an audience.

However, just because the main purpose of doing live therapy demonstrations is an educational one as reviewed above, it should not be forgotten that the person who has volunteered has done so, not only to further their education and that of their audience peers but also to seek help for themself. To reiterate a point that I made in the Introduction, I am only prepared to do a live therapy demonstration with a volunteer who is seeking help for a genuine current issue and one that they are prepared to discuss in front of an audience. Given this, I am acutely aware of the second purpose of doing live therapy demonstrations, which is a therapeutic one.

In sum, I want to offer the volunteer some help so that at the end of the day they are pleased that they volunteered for the session. In doing this, I am also acutely aware of the public nature of the session and I will take care to check with the person at various junctures whether they are prepared to discuss potentially sensitive matters in front of the audience. I am frequently surprised what volunteers are prepared to discuss and it is perhaps this fact that leads members of the watching audience to express the view that the volunteer has been brave for discussing what they have chosen to discuss.

The Importance of Realistic Expectations

I mentioned towards the end of the Introduction that I will discuss in this book the two types of live therapy demonstrations that I do: (a) demonstrations of REBT which are informed by my work in single-session therapy (SST) and b) demonstrations of SST that are informed by my work in REBT and by other approaches to therapy. You will note the different emphases in these different types of live therapy demonstrations. However, in both, I hold realistic expectations about what I can and cannot do in a live therapy demonstration. I also make this clear with a volunteer if they have unrealistically high or low expectations of what they can derive from the conversation.

What I think I can do in a live therapy demonstration is to help the volunteer take away something from our conversation that will make a difference to their life going forward. What I cannot do is to facilitate radical change in the person in such a short period of time. What is important is that the volunteer and I share realistic expectations of what they can achieve from the session. Indeed, it is unlikely that the person would volunteer if they thought that they would not benefit from doing so.

One of the features of doing live therapy demonstrations is that the conversations that I have with volunteers are the only occasions that I will meet them. Sometimes a volunteer will email me to let me know what use they have made of what we discussed, but I do not invite such contact. Indeed, live therapy demonstrations can be regarded as planned 'one-off' forms of single-session therapy. In this sense they differ from single-session therapy where the intention is to help the person with what they have come for but where more help is available if the person needs it (Dryden, 2021a). As a consequence, it is not clear what volunteers get from taking part in live therapy demonstration sessions.

Possible Therapeutic Factors

When considering what they do find helpful it is likely that different features of the live therapy demonstration are likely to be helpful for different volunteers. Having said this and in the absence of data indicating what volunteers actually find helpful about participating in live therapy demonstrations, my view is that the following are helpful factors (Dryden, 2018). I will relate these factors to the four domains of the working alliance (Dryden, 2011) which I will discuss more fully in Principle 2.

RELATIONSHIP FACTORS

These factors are related to the *bond* domain of the working alliance (see Principle 3 and Dryden, 2011).

- Being understood by the therapist
- Being accepted by the therapist
- Having their problem being taken seriously by the therapist
- The therapist not being shocked by the problem

FACTORS RELATING TO UNDERSTANDING

These factors are related to the *views* domain of the working alliance (see Principle 3 and Dryden, 2011).

- Understanding what one can change and what one cannot change

- Finding the framework offered by the therapist to understand their problem useful
- Finding the framework offered by the therapist to address their problem helpful
- Seeing that one has a choice of holding an unhelpful attitude or a helpful attitude
- Understanding the factors that one has been using to deal with the problem that, in fact, serve to maintain the problem

FACTORS RELATING TO GOALS

These factors are related to the *goals* domain of the working alliance (see Principle 3 and Dryden, 2011).

- Agreeing on a realistic and achievable goal with the therapist that concerns one's feelings and behaviours
- Agreeing on a goal that helps the person deal constructively with the adversity

CHANGE FACTORS

There are numerous change factors listed in the therapy literature. I think that the following may be particularly pertinent to live therapy demonstrations. These factors are best related to the *tasks* domain of the working alliance (see Principle 3 and Dryden, 2011).

- Engaging emotionally in the conversation
- Committing oneself to developing a helpful attitude and in particular to acting in ways that support the development of this attitude
- Choosing to face adversity and not to avoid it
- Choosing to face internal experience and not to avoid it
- Bearing disturbed emotions and being willing to experience them
- Bearing discomfort in the service of one's goals
- Bearing problematic states such as uncertainty and lack of control
- Accepting oneself as fallible
- Accepting oneself for one's original problem
- Accepting others as human
- Accepting negative aspects of life
- Putting matters into a broader perspective
- Changing one's distorted inferences
- Rehearsing new attitudes and/or new behaviours in the session
- Changing behaviour
- Being able to disclose one's problem in front of others
- Hearing similar stories from others in the audience and getting a sense of universality
- Being prepared to experiment with changing one's behaviour to elicit a healthier response from others

So far, I have discussed the therapeutic benefit that a volunteer may derive from engaging in a live therapy demonstration with me. While I do not also have in mind the purpose of providing therapy for members of the watching audience, it also happens that some members of the audience do benefit in this regard. Some say that they could relate one of their problems to a problem with which I was helping the volunteer. As I discussed the volunteer's issue the audience member was able to apply what I was saying to the volunteer to their own problem and derive help from doing so. This was a point that Albert Ellis would often make about the live therapy demonstrations he used to give at his 'Friday Night Workshop' event (see Ellis & Joffe, 2002).

The Entertainment Purpose of Live Therapy Demonstrations

The third purpose of live therapy demonstrations is to entertain the watching audience. I regard this purpose as less vital than the other two that I have discussed, but important nevertheless. In my view, if an audience is engaged while watching live therapy demonstrations then they will derive more educational benefit from them than if they are not engaged.

The use of humour largely achieves the entertaining purpose of my work in doing live therapy demonstrations. There are several functions of my humour in these demonstrations. While I use it to put the volunteer at their ease and to help the person stand back and take a humorous look at some important aspect of their problematic functioning, for the present discussion I would say that humour helps to involve the audience through its ability to entertain.

*

In this opening principle, I have discussed my three purposes when carrying out live therapy demonstrations. Such demonstrations are largely educational in nature in that they take place in an educational and training context and I do them to exemplify a particular way of working with clients. They are also therapeutic in purpose since I am directly trying to help volunteers with the emotional problems that they have chosen to discuss with me. An unintended, but welcome consequence of these demonstrations is that some members of the audience derive therapeutic benefit as well as educational benefit from watching them. Finally, and perhaps less vitally, I do strive to entertain the audience mainly through my use of humour for an engaged audience is likely to derive more educational benefit from watching live therapy demonstrations than a non-engaged audience.

In the next principle, I will discuss the role of contextual variables when considering live therapy demonstrations.

PRINCIPLE 2

The Context of Live Therapy Demonstrations

Live therapy demonstrations are best viewed within the context in which they occur. My own practice on which this book is based is not to do live therapy demonstrations on ongoing training programmes. Thus, I used to be programme director for the two-year part-time MSc in Rational Emotive Behaviour Therapy that was run at Goldsmiths University of London and did not do live demonstrations of REBT on that course. For me this was an issue of professional boundaries. My view was that it would have been inappropriate for me to serve as a therapist to any of my students, albeit in the form of a live therapy demonstration, since we had a tutor–student relationship and to also have a therapist–client relationship would have been a violation of professional ethics since I would have been having a dual relationship with the students concerned.

Consequently, this book describes live therapy demonstrations done within the context of brief training workshops where the issue of having dual relationships does not arise. Before the coronavirus pandemic, my live therapy demonstrations would have all taken place in a face-to-face training setting. The pandemic changed all this and, at the time of writing (May 2021), for the last year, all of my live therapy demonstrations have taken place online (over Zoom, Teams or Ring Central). In this chapter, I will discuss the face-to-face and online contexts of these demonstration sessions and will also discuss the recruitment of volunteers.

The Context of Live Therapy Demonstrations: An Overview

I do live therapy demonstrations in three different contexts. The first context is on training workshops either on SST or REBT which last anywhere from half-a-day to three days. Here, my demonstrations occur after I have presented material on the theory and practice of SST or REBT and want to show how the ideas that I have presented can be implemented in practice. The number of demonstrations that I will do will depend on how long the training event is. The longer the training event, the more demonstrations I will do. After each demonstration, the audience is invited to pose questions to both myself and the volunteer.

The second context is two-hour events on REBT or SST. Here, in the first hour I give a presentation on a topic such as anxiety, procrastination or guilt and then in the second hour I will do two live demonstration sessions with volunteers. Again, the audience is invited to ask questions after each session.

The third context is hour-long events where I just give two or three live therapy demonstrations and again after each session questions are directed to me and to the volunteer.

The Audience

Given the nature of the contexts that I have presented above, for the trainings that last a half a day or longer, it is likely that the people who attend these events are therapists, counsellors, those occupying other roles in the helping professions or students in these areas. For the trainings that last for one hour or two hours again, probably, most of the attendees are drawn for this group, but people who are not helping professionals or students may also attend these shorter events. These people may have an interest in REBT or SST or are friends or relatives of the professional/student attendees and attend either out of interest or specifically to volunteer to get help from a live therapy demonstration. In this book, I refer to these attendees as 'the audience'. It is from this group that people volunteer to be 'clients' in the live therapy demonstrations.

The Principle of Confidentiality

At some point before I do my live therapy demonstrations, I ask the audience to treat in confidence what the volunteer discusses with me. I tell the group that I do not mind if they discuss my work as a therapist in such a demonstration, but they should refrain from mentioning anything that the volunteer discusses. If the training event is occurring in person, I ask the audience to stand up and assert their agreement with this principle of confidentiality by sitting down. This is an active way that each member of the audience can show that they agree to abide by this principle. If the training event is occurring online, I say that I will assume that everyone in attendance will agree to abide by this principle unless they assert to the contrary. I then give a space for anyone to come forward and say that they are not prepared to do so. I have not had anyone do this, but should this occur, I would ask the person to agree not to watch the live therapy demonstration part of the training event.

Questions from the Audience

Once a live therapy demonstration has finished, the audience plays an important role in the process by directing to me and the volunteer. I will discuss this more fully in Principle 7.

The Volunteers

In this book I refer to a person who comes forward to seek help from me in a live therapy demonstration as a volunteer. A volunteer is defined as 'a person who freely offers to take part in an enterprise or undertake a task'.[3] Before a person volunteers to take part in a live therapy demonstration, I make the following points clear concerning what I am looking for from a volunteer. Thus, I ask a person to step forward if:

- *They have a current problem or issue for which they are genuinely seeking help.* It is important that the person has not made up a problem that they do not have or presents a problem that they had in the past but no longer have. It is also important that the person does not assume the role of a client that they are currently seeing or have seen in the past.

- *They are prepared to discuss the issue with me in front of an audience as described above.* A person who is considering volunteering to take part in a live therapy demonstration should ideally think about the issue that they wish to talk about and where the discussion may lead. They should only volunteer if they are

---

[3] This definition is taken from Oxford Languages.

prepared to discuss the issue with me while knowing that an audience will be watching them do so.

In addition to these two points, a person needs to be informed of other relevant information before they decide to volunteer. For example, my workshops in which the live therapy demonstrations occur are recorded for later review. If this is the case, then the person needs to know this before they agree to step forward. Also, in this circumstance, if it is the case, then I will agree with the organisers of the event that should the person later decide that they are not happy for the session that I have had with them to be shown later, their wish should be respected. If a recording is to be used for any other purpose, then, the volunteer's written informed consent should be obtained at a later date. For example, I have published several books that contain actual transcripts of live therapy demonstration sessions and before including a transcript in the book, I obtain the person's written agreement to do so (see Dryden, 2018, 2019a). In such a circumstance I give the person the opportunity of choosing the name that they wish to be known by in the transcript and I send them the transcript so that they know what will appear in the book. They can suggest any modifications to the transcript that protects their confidentiality. This transcript will also include my comments on salient parts of the demonstration session which are not open for modification by the volunteer as they are my reflections.

Volunteer Recruitment

There are several ways in which volunteers for live therapy demonstrations can be recruited.

ON THE DAY

When most training workshops occurred in person, pre Covid-19, the most frequent way in which I recruited volunteers was on the day. I would begin the workshop saying that at some point during the training I would be doing live therapy demonstrations. I would outline the criteria for volunteering (see above) and ask that anybody wishing to volunteer should see me in one of the breaks. When a person approached me to volunteer, I would accept their request. Sometimes they would ask me if I thought that their issue was suitable. In such cases, I would ask them to give me a brief overview of their issue, but invariably I said that I could work with it.

Even after Covid, in most training events, I would recruit the volunteer on the day, but there would be no opportunity for the person to check with me that their issue was appropriate to discuss during the live therapy demonstration.

BEFOREHAND

On some training workshops, the organisers prefer to recruit volunteers in advance of the event. This may be because they wish to protect a volunteer's wellbeing, or it may be because they want to avoid the situation where nobody volunteers – which incidentally has never happened to me.

Currently, I do weekly REBT-based live therapy demonstrations for the REBT Facebook Group where I interview two or three people during the live hour-long transmission. The organiser and I agreed that he would recruit the volunteers in advance since time constraints preclude from recruiting volunteers on the day. I asked Matt Walters, the group's organiser to tell me what guides his selection process. This is what he wrote:

I always meet with the volunteers the day before our sessions on the Sunday by Zoom. The volunteers either come from adverts on the group itself, or adverts that are placed on other cognitive-behaviour therapy Facebook groups. There are also some people on the REBT Facebook group who look out for volunteers and will often refer them to me.

When I meet with the people on Sunday I check to see if they have seen a 'Windy Dryden Live!' therapy demonstration before. Even if they are familiar, I would go over what the demonstration involves, making sure that they are aware that it will be played on the REBT group via Facebook live, that it will be taken down immediately after finishing and that anyone on the group can watch it. I ensure that they are aware that when the demonstration has finished, they may be asked questions from the audience.

I ask the person what their presenting problem is and I assess whether I think it is one that is suitable to be discussed in the context of the event. I make sure they have an emotional problem that is not too severe and that is not psychotic. I am not looking for easy volunteers for Windy, just people who are not suffering from any psychotic mental illness or who are not in the midst of a mental health crisis or experiencing domestic abuse.

The group has members from all over the world and I try and keep the volunteers as diverse as possible with respect to where they come from, their gender, and the nature of their problems, but this isn't always possible.

Windy often knows almost nothing about the volunteers before meeting them, although I give him a very rough outline as to what they may present.

As this group has followers from around the world and because it is a training event, I also ensure that I can understand the person that their command of the English language is adequate.

I make sure the volunteer has not had single session therapy with Windy before, unless he has specifically asked for them to return which he very occasionally does.

Finally, I ensure that the person understands the need to be somewhere quiet where they will not be disturbed during the hour of the event and that they can use a desktop or laptop for the call.

Face-to-Face vs Online Live Therapy Demonstrations

A seismic shift in the delivery of therapy and therapy training services occurred after the onset of Covid-19 and when this happened, all of my live therapy demonstrations went online. I note the following differences between working in these different media.

- When training is offered online, this means that people from outside the UK can attend virtually and thus people who volunteer to take part in live therapy demonstrations can come from across world. For example, half the volunteers for my REBT-based demonstrations on the REBT Facebook group come from India. The difference in culture is reflected in the type of problems volunteers bring to the sessions. For example, volunteers from India bring more inter-generational family problems than volunteers from the UK.
- In some cases, communication is easier in face-to-face demonstrations due to the

instability of wi-fi connectivity. This can be particularly the case with volunteers from abroad who use unstable wi-fi connections.

• Given that audience members can be asked to turn off their screens while watching the demonstrations online, both the volunteer and I are less aware of the presence of the audience than we would be in face-to-face work. This sometimes has a positive effect on some volunteers who would otherwise be adversely affected by the presence of an audience present in the same room.

The Recording and the Transcript

Whenever, I do a live therapy demonstration with a volunteer with their permission I record the session and have it transcribed later. I do this for two reasons. First, listening to a demonstration session and reading the transcript enables me to reflect on my work and improve upon it. Second, I am prepared to send the volunteer a copy of the recording and transcript on request. These materials help the person to review what we discussed and serve as a reminder for the person, if one is needed, of the main takeaway from the session and how this can be implemented (see Principle 7).

*

Live therapy demonstrations do not take place in a vacuum and in this principle, I have discussed certain salient features of the context in which they occur. In the following principle, I will present and discuss three frameworks which guide my work in conducting these demonstrations. These are: the working alliance, single-session thinking and REBT's ABC framework. Understanding these frameworks will help you to make sense of my interventions that I make in live therapy demonstrations that I will discuss in Principles 4–7.

Three Frameworks That Guide My Work in Live Therapy Demonstrations

Introduction

As I explained in the book's Introduction, I will be discussing two types of live therapy demonstrations that I conduct in the course of the training events that I present. When the training event focuses on Single-Session Therapy (SST), in my live therapy demonstrations I am guided mainly by single-session thinking but will also draw upon a number of therapeutic approaches, the main one being Rational Emotive Behaviour Therapy. By contrast when the training event focuses on Rational Emotive Behaviour Therapy, in my live therapy demonstrations, I am guided mainly by REBT but will also draw upon single-session thinking. While the emphases of these two types of live therapy demonstrations are different, there is also a significant amount of overlap and to that end I discuss the frameworks which underpin both in this principle. Also, in both types of live therapy demonstrations, I am guided by the working alliance framework that was developed by Bordin (1979) to which I later contributed (Dryden, 2006, 2011). I will begin by discussing the latter before presenting the other two frameworks: single-session thinking and the *ABCDEs* of REBT.

Before I discuss these guiding frameworks, please note that I do *not* have all this information in the front of my mind when conducting a live therapy demonstration. Rather, I see the information as a store of implicit knowledge which comes to my mind at different stages of a demonstration session. Please bear this point in mind as you read the rest of the book.

The Working Alliance Framework

'How do you develop a therapeutic relationship with a client in a single session of therapy?' This is one of the most frequently asked questions about SST to which I am called upon to respond. When I answer this question, I make reference to the working alliance framework developed by Ed Bordin (1979) and I will do so here because I have this framework in mind when I conduct a live therapy demonstration.

Bordin argued that effective therapy is likely to occur when the *bond* between therapist and client is strong, the two work together to achieve the client's *goal* and the *tasks* that both implement tasks in the service of the client's goal are effective and can be mutually understood. To these three components, I added a fourth component known as *views* (Dryden, 2006, 2011). These are understandings of salient aspects of the therapeutic process held by therapist and client. Effective therapy is more likely to occur when these understandings are shared by the two protagonists than when they are not.

Let me briefly describe which aspects of the alliance I particularly keep in mind during a live therapy demonstration.

Bonds

When I am conducting a live therapy demonstration, I have it in mind[4] that I want to show the person that I am keen to help them, that I will work hard to do so and that I will invite the person to join me in this regard. I strive to be transparent in explaining what I can do and what I cannot do during the course of the demonstration. When the volunteer nominates a problem, I keep in mind the importance of showing them that I understand their experience of this problem and that I accept them as an ordinary human being in their struggle to deal with their issue. As Rogers (1957) noted many years ago, what is important here is the person's experience of my

---

[4] When I use the term 'in mind' in this principle, I mean that it is at the back of my mind and comes to the front of my mind if something happens in the conversation that requires my attention.

empathy, genuineness and acceptance rather than any objective markers of these 'core conditions'.

Goals

Given the single-session nature of a live therapy demonstration, I keep in mind the importance of encouraging the person to set a session goal which I hope will help the person to 'kick-start' the change process. I note to myself that while I may ask the person about what they want to achieve from the outset I may need to return to this issue as the session unfolds. I also keep in mind the difference between a session goal (that which the person wants to achieve at the end of our conversations) and a problem-related goal (which would indicate to them that they would be handling the adversity with which they have a problem in a constructive manner). Using this difference, I will remind myself to look for an opportunity to help the volunteer to see the relationship between achieving their session goal and their problem-related goal.

As Bordin (1979) noted, the most important aspect with respect to goals in therapy is that the therapist and client agree that they are working towards the same objective. I will keep this point very much in mind and will explicitly check that this is the case during my conversation with the volunteer, particularly if I am unclear that this is the case.

Views

As I mentioned above, I introduced a fourth component of the working alliance that I termed 'views' because I considered that this was an important aspect of the alliance that was absent from Bordin's (1979) original conceptualisation (Dryden, 2006, 2011). With respect to a live therapy demonstration, such views relate to the various understandings that the volunteer and I have pertaining to the conversation we are having that is at the heart of this demonstration. Thus, I hold in mind the following 'views' and will check these out as needed during the demonstration:

- What does the volunteer understand about the demonstration and why we are having it?
- What does the person think can be realistically achieved from having the conversation with me?
- In the person's view what are the important factors that account for their problem and what factors does the person think need to be present if they are to deal effectively with their problem?

The healing aspect of this fourth component of the working alliance lies in the shared nature of these understandings between me and the volunteer.

If I am carrying out a live therapy demonstration on REBT where the explicit focus is on this approach to therapy, I will keep in mind the importance of checking with the person what they think of my REBT-based view of their problem and what they need to do to solve it.

Tasks

As noted by Bordin (1979), tasks are activities and procedures that therapists and clients engage in to help the clients reach their goals. The more the two protagonists understand one another's tasks and agree to implement their own, the greater the positive impact on client outcome.

With respect to the task domain of the alliance in live therapy demonstrations of SST, I keep in mind to ask the volunteer what they have done in the past that may help them deal effectively with their nominated problem. I will also keep in mind a range of therapeutic procedures that I may engage in to help the person in this respect. When I am demonstrating REBT, I keep in mind a range of REBT-based activities that I will draw upon depending on what the volunteer decides to discuss in the conversation. I also think about potential REBT-based tasks that the volunteer may use to help themself after the session has finished.

While there have been no studies relating the working alliance to live therapy demonstrations, there has been research that shows that those who benefit from single-session therapy have a better alliance with their therapists than those who do not benefit from SST (Simon, Imel, Ludman & Steinfeld, 2012).

Single-Session Thinking

Whether I am doing a live therapy demonstration of single-session therapy (SST) or of Rational Emotive Behaviour Therapy (REBT), I am guided by single-session thinking (also known as the single-session mindset (Hoyt, Young & Rycroft, 2020). Indeed, whatever I am demonstrating, I am mindful of the fact that I will only be speaking to the volunteer on one occasion and thus the following components of single-session therapy are never far from my mind as I conduct the session.

Realistic Expectations for What Can Be Achieved from a Live Demonstration Session

Expectation is a powerful therapeutic factor (Constantino, Glass, Arnkoff, Ametrano & Smith, 2011). However, it is important that the volunteer has a realistic expectation of what can be achieved from a live therapy demonstration and I keep this point clearly in mind as the conversation unfolds.

The Power of 'Now'

Single-session thinking encourages me to think that all we have is 'now' and thus to be mindful of using the time I have with the person as productively as possible.

Less Is More

When I supervise therapists in their single-session work, one of the issues that they struggle with is the urge to give their clients as much to take away as possible given that they might not see the clients again. As I noted in a companion volume in this book series (Dryden, 2021a), this can be a recipe for disaster in that the risk is that a client may leave 'feeling' overloaded and takes away nothing from the process. Single-session thinking teaches us that 'less is more' and often if a volunteer takes away just one thing that is meaningful that they can use afterwards they are more than happy to have participated in the conversation with me (Keller & Papasan, 2012). So 'less is more' is a concept that is at the back of my mind as I conduct a live therapy demonstration.

The Importance of Being Client-Centred

In conventional clinical thinking, the therapist assesses the client's problem and suggests a way forward based on that assessment. With this mindset, therapy is driven by the therapist. In single-session thinking, the client determines the problem and suggests what they are looking for from the session. With this mindset, the live therapy demonstration is driven by the volunteer. Being client-centred does not mean that I will refrain from sharing my own ideas with the volunteer. However, when I do so, I will first determine that the person is interested in my views before sharing them.

Engage the Client Quickly Through the Work

In traditional therapy, treatment is based on such procedures as conducting a full assessment, history taking and carrying out a case formulation. Obviously, there is no time to do these things in live therapy demonstrations. Instead, the priority is to engage the volunteer quickly and this is done through the work itself. If I can convey my keenness to help the person and invite them to join me as an active participant in the process, this is usually sufficient to engage them, and I have this principle in mind as I begin the conversation.

Think of the Volunteer's Takeaway at the Outset

I find it useful to keep in mind at the beginning of a live therapy demonstration what the person would like to takeaway from the session that would make a difference to them. With this idea in mind, I look for a suitable time to ask the person for their 'hoped-for' takeaway.

Deciding on the Best Helping Stance with the Volunteer

Most of the time, a person volunteers for a live therapy demonstration wanting to discuss an emotional problem that they have for which they are seeking some kind of resolution. However, at other times a volunteer seeks greater clarity on an issue without necessarily wanting a solution. Consequently, I keep in mind the idea that I need to assume the best helping stance to meet the volunteer's goal in having a conversation with me. I will discuss this further in Principle 4.

Agree a Focus with the Volunteer

In most live therapy demonstrations, where the person is seeking some help with an emotional problem, it is important to create a focus for the session which will guide the volunteer's and my search for an effective resolution to this problem or issue. This is particularly important when the person mentions several problems or several different features of one problem. Thus, I keep the word 'focus' in mind at the outset of a live therapy demonstration.

Keep on Track

Once I have agreed a focus with a volunteer, then I keep it in mind that I need to keep the conversation on track or to change tack if the volunteer decides that some other focus is more meaningful to them as the conversation unfolds. I keep in mind the need to check that the person is discussing what *they* want to discuss.

Keep Up a Good Therapeutic Pace and Stop When Finished

As the conversation proceeds, I will get a sense of the pace at which I need to work to engage the person. I also keep it is mind that we finish when the person is satisfied that they have gotten what they have come for. This means that a live demonstration session does not last for a fixed time agreed beforehand.

The Importance of Being Clear and Fostering Clarity

I keep in mind that it is important for there to be clear communication between me and the volunteer. This means that I need to check that I am being clear and also that I am understanding what the volunteer is saying. If not, I keep in mind the need to seek clarification.

Make an Emotional Impact

In my view, an effective live therapy demonstration is one in which engages the volunteer's 'head and heart'. Thus, I will keep in mind the need to make use of opportunities to make an emotional impact on the volunteer.

Identify and Make Use of the Volunteer's Strengths

An important aspect of single-session work is identifying a volunteer's strengths and encouraging them to make use of these internal factors as they address their problem. I keep this point in mind during the live therapy demonstration.

Encourage the Person to Use Environmental Resources

Similarly, single-session thinking prompts me to encourage the volunteer during the session to think of their environment as a potential source of assistance in the solution of their problem.

Identify and Make Use of the Volunteer's Previous Attempts to Deal with the Problem

If a volunteer nominates a problem they would like me to help them solve, I keep in mind the idea that it is useful for us both to know what they have done before in attempting to deal with the problem. This information helps us discover what we can build on and what we can discard as we search together for a solution.

Encourage the Volunteer to Summarise Periodically

Therapists often summarise what their clients have discussed as a way of synthesizing what they have both been discussing. By contrast, single-session thinking suggests that I ask the volunteer to do this instead as this encourages them to stay active in the process and to be clear with themself and with me what they are learning from the session. While conducting a live demonstration session, I keep this point in mind particularly when a substantial piece of work has been done and also at the end of the conversation.

Negotiate a Solution

Particularly when a volunteer would like help with a nominated problem, single-session thinking encourages me to work with the person to develop a solution potentially drawing upon everything we have discussed up to that point. I will discuss this in greater detail in Principle 6.

Encourage the Volunteer to Rehearse the Solution

If I have helped a volunteer to develop a solution, single-session thinking encourages me to keep in mind the possibility of asking the person to rehearse the solution, if practicable, since this enables the person to 'road-test' the solution and make any necessary adjustments to it.

Helping the Volunteer to Develop an Action Plan

If the solution is one that needs to be acted upon, single-session thinking suggests that I encourage the volunteer to make an action plan to do so.

End the Conversation Well

In the same way as it is important for me to begin the conversation well, single-session thinking suggests that it is important that I end it well. I will discuss this issue more fully in Principle 7.

The *ABCDEs* of Rational Emotive Behaviour Therapy

The third framework that I keep in mind, particularly when I carry out REBT-based live therapy demonstrations, is REBT's *ABCDE* framework (see Dryden, 2021b for a full discussion of this framework). Here is a summary of the *ABCDE* framework.

> *A = Adversity*
> *B = Basic Attitudes*
> *C = Consequences of B*
> *D = Dialectical Examination of B*
> *E = Effects of D*

Here are the main points of this framework that I keep in mind when I am doing a live demonstration of REBT.

- I agree a focus with the volunteer which will usually be an emotional problem.
- I ask the volunteer to provide a specific example of this problem.
- I identify the person's main disturbed emotion and associated behaviour and thinking at C.
- I use C to find the person's major adversity at A. This is what the person is most disturbed about.
- According to REBT, it is the person's rigid and extreme basic attitudes at B that they hold towards the adversity at A that largely determine their problematic response at C and not A itself. I help the person to identify which rigid and extreme attitudes they hold towards

the adversity that account for their problem and to identify which alternative flexible and non-extreme attitudes they could hold towards the same adversity that would provide the attitudinal solution to their problem.

- I then invite the volunteer to stand back and examine these two sets of attitudes at D^5 helping them to choose the flexible/non-extreme attitudes to take forward as the attitudinal solution to their emotional problem.
- I then help the person then to a plan to implement this solution going forward which are the effects at E of D.

*

In this principle I have elucidated the three main frameworks that guide the live therapy demonstrations that I do.

Once again, I want to stress that I don't act on all these points in a single demonstration and I do not keep them all at the forefront of my mind either. However, the points that comprise these frameworks are at the back of my mind and when relevant I bring

---

[5] D stands for 'dialectical' which means finding a resolution between two opposite positions. Rigid/extreme and flexible/non-extreme attitudes represent such opposite positions.

them to the front of my mind and act on them. In Appendix 1 and Appendix 2 I present two transcripts of live therapy demonstration where I make clear the thinking that guided my side of the conversations.

In the next principle, I will discuss how to initiate live therapy demonstrations and discuss several ways of doing so.

PRINCIPLE 4

Getting Live Therapy Demonstrations off to a Good Start and Co-Creating a Focus

In this principle, I will first review what I have already said about recruiting a volunteer, then I will briefly comment on what happens once a volunteer has come forward, but before we begin our conversation before outlining possible ways of initiating a live therapy demonstration. Then I will discuss the importance of creating a focus with the volunteer.

Before the Person Has Volunteered

You will recall from Principle 2 that I discussed who should ideally volunteer for a live therapy demonstration and the differences between prior recruitment of a volunteer and 'on the day' recruitment. In beginning a live therapy demonstration, I make reference to the context in which the person has volunteered as I will show below. Before doing so, let me reiterate the information that I think somebody needs to know about before they decide to volunteer for the session.

Thus, I or a colleague who has the responsibility to recruit a volunteer will say something like:

> 'Please volunteer for the live therapy demonstration if:
>
> (a) You have a genuine, current problem, concern or issue[6] for which you are seeking help.
> (b) You are prepared to discuss this problem, concern or issue in front of an audience[7] of your peers.
> (c) You are prepared to answer questions from the audience.'

Once the Person Has Volunteered, but Before We Begin

I will now assume that the person has volunteered, and we are sitting together either in the same room or on the online platform that is being used.

---

[6] I have learned over the years that some people resonate more to the 'problem' in this context while others prefer the use of a term such as 'issue' or 'concern'. As such, I generally use all three in my recruiting statement.

[7] In pre-pandemic times, this would largely be an audience that was present in the room with the volunteer and me. However, increasingly, delegates had the option of watching the training workshop and thus the live therapy demonstration online synchronously or at a later date. During the pandemic, workshops have been only conducted online with synchronous or later viewing. The recruiting statement would reflect the prevailing situation.

If members of the audience are present in the room with us, I usually ask them to be silent through the demonstration and even refrain from whispering to the person next to them since such noise can be heard and is generally disruptive.

If the members of the audience are online, I ask the organisers at that point to shut off everyone's cameras, mute everyone and organise the online chat so that neither I nor the volunteer can see it. I find it very disruptive to see comments come up in the online chat facility while I am carrying out a live therapy demonstration.

Beginning the Live Therapy Demonstration

Over the years, I have experimented with several ways of beginning a live therapy demonstration.

When the Person Has Been Recruited in Advance

If a person has been recruited in advance to take part in the live therapy demonstration then one way of initiating the session is to acknowledge that fact and use it as a starting off point:

Q: *When you were asked to take part in this live therapy demonstration, what did the person who invited you tell about what was involved?*

I will then respond to whatever the person says.

When the Person Volunteers on the Day

When the person has volunteered on the day, I may begin with their decision to do so.

Q: *When you decided to volunteer for this live therapy demonstration what prompted you to do so?*

Again, I will respond to whatever the person says.

Questions about the Purpose of the Conversation

A different way of beginning a live therapy demonstration involves me asking the volunteer a question about the purpose of the conversation from their perspective.

Q: *From your perspective, what is the purpose of our conversation today?*

If the person has an unrealistic expectation of the session's purpose, then I will have a very early opportunity to deal with this and point out what I can do and what I can't do.

Questions about the Problem, Concern or Issue

As noted above, my call for volunteers asks for someone to come forward if they have a genuine, current problem, concern or issue for which they are seeking help. Given this, I can begin the conversation thus:

Q: *What problem, concern or issue would you like to discuss with me?*

Q: *What problem, concern or issue would you like me to help you with?*

Questions about the Person's Goals

Instead of being problem focused, an alternative is to begin the live therapy demonstration by being goal focused. Taking this stance, I could ask:

Q: *What would you like to achieve by talking with me today?*

Q: *What would you like to take away from our conversation that would make it worthwhile that you volunteered today?*

Questions that Focus on Help

Another way of beginning live therapy demonstrations is to focus on the concept of help. For example:

Q: *How can I be most helpful to you today?*

Q: *What help would you like from me today?*

These questions allow the person to specify the help that they want the therapist to give them, what they want help with or both.

Open Invitations to Begin

Some people who do live therapy demonstrations prefer to begin these sessions in a more open-ended manner. These therapists, particularly those working from a person centred perspective, are uncomfortable with a 'problem focus' way of beginning live therapy demonstrations and prefer to give the person a more open invitation to begin. Here is how Carl Rogers initiated his live therapy demonstration of what was then known as client-centred therapy[8] with Gloria in the first of the 'Three Approaches to Psychotherapy' film series.[9]

Rogers: (Rogers stands as Gloria enters.) Good morning.

Gloria: Hello, Dr. Rogers.

Rogers: I'm Dr. Rogers, you must be Gloria.

Gloria: Yes, I am.

Rogers: Won't you have a chair? Now then, we have half an hour together, and I really don't know what we will be able to make of it but uh I

---

[8] Now known as person centred therapy.
[9] In this series of films entitled 'Three Approaches to Psychotherapy I', 'Gloria' (not her real name) is interviewed by three therapists, Carl Rogers, Fritz Perls and Albert Ellis.

hope we can make something of it. I'd be glad to know whatever concerns you.

[*Some person centred practitioners are not happy with the Rogers' use of the word 'concerns' here and suggest that an even more open invitation would have been: 'I'd be glad to know whatever you wish to discuss with me.'*]

Gloria: Well, right now I'm nervous, but I feel more comfortable the way you are talking in a low voice and I don't feel like you'll be so harsh on me. But, ah ...

Rogers: I hear the tremor in your voice so I know you are...

[*Gloria discloses her nervousness, but notes that Rogers's voice tone is putting her at ease and he conveys understanding by recognising the nervousness in her voice.*]

The advantage of the open invitation is that it does not constrain the person in what they want to discuss. However, it may lead them to think that they have more time to put matters into a historical context, for example, than they do.

In contrast, consider how Albert Ellis, the originator of what was then known as Rational-

Emotive Therapy[10] began the live demonstration of his approach with Gloria.

Ellis:	Well, Gloria, Dr. Ellis. You want to…
Gloria:	How do you do, Dr. Ellis?
Ellis:	…be seated please.
Gloria:	Okay.
Ellis:	Well, would you like to tell me what is bothering you most.

[*As REBT is a problem-focused therapy, Ellis's opening question is consistent with his approach which is very similar to my own. He invites Gloria to select the problem that bothers her most.*]

Gloria: (sighs) Hmmm…Well…I think the things that I would like to talk to you the most about are adjusting to my single life…

[*While Ellis invites Gloria to discuss what she is most bothered about, she responds by saying what she most wants to talk about. However, a context has been delineated which will later become the focus of the session.*]

To complete the trilogy, here is how Fritz Perls, the originator of Gestalt Therapy began the live therapy demonstration of his approach with Gloria.

---

[10] Now known as Rational Emotive Behaviour Therapy.

Perls:	We are going to have an interview for half an hour.
Gloria:	(long pause and lights a cigarette) By the way, I'm scared.
Perls:	You say you are scared, but you're smiling. I don't understand how one can be scared and smile at the same time.

> [*In this beginning, Perls does not introduce himself. He initiates the conversation with a fact – that their interview will last for half an hour – and his response to Gloria's first statement begins therapy immediately in a way that is consistent with Gestalt Therapy.*]

As can be seen, there is no one approach to begin a live therapy demonstration and to some extent, practitioners begin in ways that are consistent with their orientation to therapy.

Asking for Permission to Interrupt the Person

One of the things that therapists generally find it difficult to do is to interrupt clients. This is due to such ideas that 'it is rude to interrupt the client', 'it takes the session away from where the client wants to go' and 'I would be intruding on the client's process'. While they may be some truth to all these views, from the perspective of the therapist conducting a live therapy demonstration, they obscure the importance and value of interrupting the volunteer. Time is of the essence in conducting a live therapy demonstration and if the therapist is going to help the volunteer in such limited time, they need to be able to interrupt the person in order to keep them both on track.

The best way I have found of interrupting the person is to first provide a rationale for doing so and then to ask for the person's permission to do so. This is best done at the earliest possible opportunity and I see it as one of my tasks at the beginning of the demonstration session. Here is an example of how I might introduce this into the conversation.

> *Windy:* Sometimes after we have agreed what to discuss in the session, I may have to bring you back to our agreed focus and I may have to interrupt you. I will attempt to do so as courteously as possible. May I have your permission to do this?
>
> *Volunteer:* Yes, that is fine. It would be helpful actually because I know that I have a tendency to go off at tangents.

I find that this is quite a common reaction to my request for permission to interrupt the person.

Co-creating a Focus

After I have initiated a live therapy demonstration, I am keen to develop a working focus with the volunteer as soon as possible. An agreed focus gives shape to the session and informs both of us concerning what we should be discussing. In my work, ideally, there are three components of a good focus: (i) a problem (issue or concern); (ii) a problem-related goal (i.e. what the person wants to achieve with respect to the problem) and (iii) a conversation-related goal (what the person wants to take away from the conversation that would make their volunteering for it worthwhile. the person). While I like to have all three components present in an agreed focus, this is not always possible. In which case, I will work with a focus that has two or even one component present. Here are some examples of agreed foci.

- *A focus based on three components*: 'I am anxious about being criticised at work. I want to be concerned, but not anxious about being criticised and I want to learn how to do this by the end of the session.'
- *A focus based on two components*: 'I am anxious about being criticised at work. I want to be concerned, but not anxious about being criticised.'

- *A focus based on one component*: 'I am anxious about being criticised at work.'

When a Focus Is Clear at the Outset and When It Is Not

Sometimes the focus is clear at the very beginning of the live therapy demonstration and at other times it becomes clear during the conversation. It is important for me to respond flexibly to whatever the person says. Here is an example of where the focus is clear at the outset.

Windy: What problem, concern or issue would you like to discuss with me?

Volunteer: I want to discuss my anxiety about being criticised at work.

Here is an example where the focus is not clear at the outset.

Windy: What problem, concern or issue would you like to discuss with me?

Volunteer: Things are not quite right in my life and I'm not sure why.

Windy: If things were right in life, what would be different for you?

[*Responding to the volunteer's vague statement, I ask a question designed to get greater specificity.*]

Volunteer: I think the main thing would be that I would look forward to going to work.

Windy: And what would be different for you to look forward to going to work?

[*The volunteer narrows the issue down to work which is a little more specific, but greater specificity is needed, hence my question.*]

Volunteer: People would not criticise my work.

Windy: How do you deal with this criticism?

[*I am aware that creating a work environment where criticism of the person does not take place is outside of our collective control, so I focus on the person's response to such criticism.*]

Volunteer: I don't deal with it well at all. I get anxious about it.

Windy: What if you felt that you could handle being criticised at work better would that make a difference to you?

Volunteer: Yes, it would.

Windy: In what way?

Volunteer: Well, I do not enjoy my work and if I felt able to deal with being criticised better, I would look forward to going to work.

[*Having ascertained that the volunteer is anxious about being criticised, I ask if dealing with criticism would help.*]

Windy: And if you looked forward to going to work, would you consider that things were right in your life?
[*This question relates to what the volunteer first said.*]

Volunteer: Well, it would make an appreciable difference

Windy: So, does it make sense for us to focus on helping you deal with criticism better in our session today?

Volunteer: Yes, it does.
[*Here an agreed focus has been reached.*]

When a Person Mentions Two or More Problems at the Outset

Sometimes when asked what they want to discuss, a volunteer may mention two or more issues. Given that there is usually insufficient time to cover more than one issue in detail, the person is asked to nominate one issue on which they would like to concentrate. Here is an example.

Windy: What problem, concern or issue would you like to discuss with me?

Volunteer: Well, I am struggling at work at the moment, my relationship with my girlfriend isn't going very well and I'm behind in my college work.

Windy: Given that we probably won't have time to deal with all of these, which one of these issues would you want to concentrate?

or

Windy: It sounds like you are facing quite a lot. If I can help you with one of these issues the resolution of which would give you most hope for the future which one would it be?

Another approach to when the person mentions more than one issue is to ask the person if there is any theme that links the issues and if there is to work with this identified as the focus. For example:

Windy: What problem, concern or issue would you like to discuss with me?

Volunteer: I am struggling at work at the moment and my relationship with my girlfriend isn't going very well.

Windy: Is there any theme that links these two issues that you can see?

Volunteer: Interesting question….(pause)…I guess it's the difficulty trouble I have dealing with criticism.

Windy: So, would if make sense for us to focus on helping you to deal with criticism today?

Volunteer: That would be good.

Windy: Would the best context to start discussing this be the work issue or the relationship issue?

Volunteer: I think the work issue.

Windy: Ok and then perhaps I can help you generalise what you learn from our discussion to dealing with criticism in your relationship?

Volunteer: That would be very useful.

As can be seen from the above dialogue, having helped the person identify a theme, I suggest that the person selects a context for our conversation of the theme and mention that I will help them to generalise their learning to the other context.

*

In this principle, I have concentrated on the beginning phase of a live therapy demonstration. Specifically, I reviewed what I say when recruiting a volunteer and what I say to the audience before I commence the session. I then discussed a variety of different ways of beginning the conversation. Then, I detailed the importance of interrupting the person to make the best use of time in the session and outlined how I introduce this issue with the person who has volunteered for the session. I concluded the principle by considering the importance of co-creating a focus for the session.

In the following principle, I will discuss the importance of understanding the problem the person wishes to discuss and the context in which it is experienced.

PRINCIPLE 5

The Importance of Understanding the Volunteer's Nominated Problem in Context

Introduction

In my experience, therapists who do live therapy demonstrations are either solution-focused (where they predominantly search for a solution to the person's problem) or problem- and solution-focused (where they seek to understand the problem before searching for a solution to it). I would describe my work as primarily problem- and solution-focused and, as such, once the volunteer and I have agreed a therapeutic focus for the session, the next step is for us both to understand the person's nominated problem[11] in context.

---

[11] I refer to the problem (concern or issue) that the person and I have agreed will be the focus of the live therapy demonstration as the person's 'nominated' problem.

Others' Work on Live Therapy Demonstrations

While other therapists do live therapy demonstrations, there is a dearth of published written material on this subject. Barber (1990) wrote a chapter on his approach to what he called 'clinical demonstrations' which he gave in workshop settings. In his chapter, he did not discuss the ideas that informed his demonstrations, but from what I can gather they were underpinned by Ericksonian Therapy.[12] However, he did discuss the early single-session work of Bloom (1981) and Talmon, Hoyt & Rosenbaum (1988) and noted that these ideas provide a good grounding to the practice of live therapy demonstrations. Of course, the field of SST has developed much since the publication of Barber's (1990) chapter as I showed in Principle 3.

Lankton & Zeig (1989) edited a collection of six demonstrations of Ericksonian Therapy which were given at training events organised by the Milton H. Erickson Foundation. Here a transcript of the session is provided followed by two commentaries on the session, one by the therapist himself and the other by one of the book's other contributors.[13] Due to the fact that this book is in a series entitled 'Ericksonian Monographs' it was clearly prepared for an audience

---

[12] Barber is a contributor to the book on Ericksonian Therapy demonstrations mentioned below.

[13] All the therapists and commentators are male.

very familiar with Ericksonian ideas. Hence, there was no attempt to explain Ericksonian Therapy in a way that would be comprehensible to a wide readership and help such readers better understand the work that was done in the published demonstrations.

My Work

In this principle I will refer to my own practice of therapy demonstrations which are very different from demonstrations of Ericksonian Therapy. Thus, I will discuss both my SST-based and REBT-based demonstrations. You will recall from the introduction that I said that my REBT-based demonstrations feature my practice of Rational Emotive Behaviour Therapy but are informed by single-session thinking and that my SST demonstrations feature my practice of single-session therapy, but are informed by a number of therapeutic orientations, the main one being REBT. Given that REBT is likely to feature in both types of live therapy demonstrations, I will begin by outlining the ABC framework that I use to inform my understanding of the person's nominated problem. Before I do this, however, I will discuss the importance of working with a specific example of the person's problem whenever practicable.

Working with an Example of the Person's Nominated Problem

I generally find it helpful to work with a specific example of the volunteer's nominated problem since doing so makes the problem come alive, as it were, and avoids the person talking about the problem generally and thus theoretically. Working with a specific example of the person's problem also increases the chances that they will be emotionally engaged in the conversation. I generally inform the person that a good specific example is one which captures all the factors involved. It would include the situation in which the problem occurred, the adversity that featured in the problem and the people involved. The person can be encouraged to select a predicted imminent example, a recent example, a typical example or a memorable example. My own preference is to work with a predicted imminent example because doing so makes it easier for the person to implement any solution which we co-create in the upcoming situation.

Using REBT's ABC Framework to Understand the Person's Nominated Problem

Particularly when I am doing a live demonstration of Rational Emotive Behaviour Therapy (REBT), I utilise REBT's ABC framework to help myself and the volunteer understand the person's nominated problem.

A = *Adversity*
B = *Basic Attitudes*
C = *Consequences of B (Emotional, Behavioural and Thinking)*

In doing so, my preference, for reasons discussed above, is to work with a specific example of the nominated problem.

Describe the Situation in Which the Problem Occurred

There is a game known as 'Cluedo'[14] where the task of players is to discover the identity of the murderer ('who'), where the murder took place ('where') and the murder weapon ('how'). The object of the game is descriptive. Similarly, my task at this point is to gain a description of the 'situation' in which the volunteer experienced the problem: who was present, where they were and what they were all doing.

---

[14] Known as 'Clue' in the USA.

Identify the Volunteer's Problem Response ('C')

As shown above, 'C' represents the emotional, behavioural and thinking elements of the volunteer's problem. Thus, after discovering the 'situation' in which the volunteer's problem occurred, my next task is to identify the components of the volunteer's problematic response in this described situation. This involves me finding out what the person was feeling, what they were doing and if necessary, what type of feeling-related thinking they were engaged in. I normally begin with the person's emotional 'C' because it is usually what has led the person to volunteer for help.

REBT is unique in the therapeutic world in making a distinction between emotions that are negative in experiential tone and largely unhealthy in effect (known as 'unhealthy negative emotions') and emotions that are negative in experiential tone and largely healthy in effect (known as 'healthy negative emotions'). This is shown on the next page.

My task is to help the volunteer to identify the *one* major UNE that featured in their problem from the grey shaded area above. Later, I will help the volunteer to set an emotional goal which will be the corresponding HNE. This represents the fact that a healthy way of responding to the adversity that features in the person's problem (to be discussed in the following section) involves that person experiencing an emotion that in negative in experiential tone, but healthy in effect.

Unhealthy Negative Emotion (HNE)	Healthy Negative Emotion (HNE)
Anxiety	Concern
Depression	Sadness
Guilt	Remorse
Shame	Disappointment
Hurt	Sorrow
Unhealthy anger	Healthy anger
Unhealthy jealousy	Healthy jealousy
Unhealthy envy	Healthy envy

Once I have helped the person to identify their major UNE, I help them to identify the behaviour and thinking that accompanied this UNE. Such behaviour is likely to be unconstructive and such thinking is likely to be highly distorted and skewed to the negative. Here, I am guided by REBT's theory of unhealthy negative emotions (see Dryden, 2022 for a full discussion of each UNE and its behavioural and thinking concomitants).

Identify the Adversity ('A') that Features in the Volunteer's Problem

After I have helped the volunteer to identify their major UNE, I use this to find what they were most disturbed about in the selected example. This constitutes the adversity which features in this problem. To do this, I use a method that I devised for this purpose which I have termed 'Windy's Magic Question' (WMQ). Here is an example of how I use it.

- I have the person focus on their disturbed emotional 'C' (e.g. 'anxiety').
- I then have them focus on the situation in which 'C' occurred (e.g. 'about to give a public presentation to a group of consultants').
- I then ask the person: *'Which ingredient could we give you to eliminate or significantly reduce 'C'?* (here, anxiety)*?* (In this case the person said: 'my mind not going blank'.) I take care that the person does not change the situation (i.e. they do not say: 'not giving the presentation').
- The opposite is probably 'A' (e.g. 'my mind going blank'), but I check by asking: *'So when you were about to give the presentation, were you most anxious about your mind going blank?'* If not, I use the question again until the person confirms what they were most anxious about in the described situation.

REB theory suggests that a person's negative emotions (both unhealthy and healthy) suggest the presence of an adversity theme which in its specific form features in the person's emotional problem. I use the following as a guide to help me identify this specific adversity.

Adversity/Theme	UNE	HNE
• Threat	Anxiety	Concern
• Loss • Failure • Undeserved plight (experienced by self or others)	Depression	Sadness
• Breaking your moral code • Failing to abide by your moral code • Hurting someone	Guilt	Remorse
• Falling very short of your ideal in a social context • Others judging you negatively	Shame	Disappointment
• The other is less invested in your relationship than you • Someone betrays you or lets you down and you think do not deserve such treatment	Hurt	Sorrow
• You or another transgresses a personal rule • Another disrespects you • Frustration	Unhealthy anger	Healthy anger
• Someone poses a threat to a valued relationship • You experience uncertainty related to this threat	Unhealthy jealousy	Healthy jealousy
• Others have what you value and lack	Unhealthy envy	Healthy envy

Identify the Person's Rigid Attitude Towards the Adversity that Underpins their Problem and Their Alternative Flexible Attitude

Once I have identified the person's 'C' (e.g. 'anxiety') and their 'A' (e.g. 'my mind going blank'), I use a technique called Windy's Review Assessment Procedure (WRAP) to identify the person's rigid attitude that REBT argues underpins their unhealthy response to the adversity emotional problem and the alternative flexible attitude that is deemed to underpin their healthy response to the same adversity. This helps them to understand the two relevant B–C connections. This technique can also be used with any extreme attitude the person may hold along with its non-extreme attitude. Here is an example of how use 'Windy's Review Assessment Procedure' (WRAP).

- I say: *'Let's review what we know and what we don't know so far.'*
- Then I say *'We know three things. First, we know that you were anxious ('C'). Second, we know that you were anxious about your mind going blank ('A'). Third, and this is an educated guess on my part, we know that it is important to you that your mind does not go blank. Am I correct?'*
- Assuming that the person confirms my hunch, note that I have has done is to identify the part of the attitude that is common to both the

person's rigid attitude and alternative flexible attitude, as we will see.

- Next, I say: *'Now let's review what we don't know. This is where I need your help. We don't know which of two attitudes your anxiety was based on. So, when you were anxious about your mind going blank was your anxiety based on Attitude 1: 'It is important to me that my mind does not go blank and therefore it must not do so'* ('Rigid attitude') *or Attitude 2: 'It is important to me that my mind does not go blank, but that does not mean that it must not do so* ('Flexible attitude')?'

- If necessary, I help the person to understand that their anxiety was based on their rigid attitude if they are unsure.

- Once the person is clear that their anxiety was based on their rigid attitude, I make and emphasize the rigid attitude-disturbed 'C' connection. Then, I ask: *'Now let's suppose instead that you had a strong conviction in Attitude 2, how would you feel about your mind going blank if you strongly believed that while it was important to you that your mind did not go blank, it did not follow that it must not do so?'*

- If necessary, I help the person to select a healthy negative emotion such as concern, if not immediately volunteered, and make and emphasize the flexible attitude-healthy 'C' connection.

- I ensure that the person clearly understands the differences between the two B–C connections.
- I help the person set concern as the emotional goal in this situation and encourage them to see that developing conviction in their flexible attitude is the best way of achieving this goal.

While I have outlined the WMQ and WRAP methods in full here, and I sometimes use them as described above, more often I use only elements of them in live therapy demonstrations, particularly if time is at a premium. Also, please note that while I use these methods most often in live demonstrations of REBT, I also use them in live demonstrations of SST when I think that the person may benefit from an REBT-based understanding of their problem.

Using SST Thinking to Understand the Person's Nominated Problem

When using SST thinking to understand the person's nominated problem, I would begin by asking the person to state the problem as they see it and then proceed by inviting them to give me their views of the factors involved in the problem. I would then ask them what makes the problem better and what makes it worse to flush out the variables that serve to maintain the problem. I would also ask the person whether they have ever expected the problem to be present and it has been absent and how they accounted for this difference.

While I may not use REBT's ABC framework explicitly in my live demonstrations of SST that are not designed to feature REBT, I may still use it as my internal guide to understand the volunteer's problem. In particular, I hold in mind the REBT view that the presence of negative emotions (both unhealthy and healthy) suggest the presence of general inference themes which may point in the person's case to the presence of the adversity that features in their nominated problem. I may ask the person if they are interested in my view of the problem. If they are, I might proceed as follows.

> *Windy:*   So, you have mentioned that you don't say 'no' to your sister-in-law when she asks you to babysit for her even though it is inconvenient for you to do because you would feel guilty if you did. Is that right?
>
> *Volunteer:* That is right.
>
> *Windy:*   And you said earlier that you would like to deal with your feelings of guilt.
>
> *Volunteer:* Yes, it is a big issue for me.
>
> *Windy:*   Would you like to hear my view on guilt?
>
> *Volunteer:* Yes, please.

Windy: Well, when a person feels guilt, they think that they have broken their moral code, fail to live up to their moral code or hurt someone. When you predict you would feel guilty about saying 'no' to your sister-in-law which of those themes do you feel guilty about?

Volunteer: Definitely upsetting her.

Windy: Apart from feeling guilty about upsetting your sister-in-law what are your options about how to respond to her upset feelings?

*

In this principle, I have discussed the importance of understanding the volunteer's problem and I have done so from the perspectives of REBT and SST. In the next principle, I will discuss building on this understanding in the search for a solution to the person's nominated problem.

PRINCIPLE 6

Facilitating Change in Live Therapy Demonstrations

In this principle, I will discuss what is the heart of giving live therapy demonstrations – helping the volunteer deal effectively with their nominated problem, concern or issue. Here, then, my focus is on facilitating change based on an understanding of the problem that I discussed in the previous principle. I will discuss, searching for a solution and how my work here is influenced by insights from SST and by insights from REBT. I will then discuss the importance of helping the person to rehearse the selected solution in the session if this is practicable. Finally, I will consider how I might help the person to implement to solution in their daily life.

The Importance of Working with Goals in Live Therapy Demonstrations

All good therapy should ideally have a direction (Cooper & Law, 2018) and in live therapy demonstrations this is set by the volunteer. In my thinking, I distinguish between two types of goals in these demonstration sessions: a goal that is related to the person's nominated problem (a 'problem-related goal') and what the person wants to take away from the session with me (a 'session goal'). Quite often a session goal suggests looking for a solution which if implemented will help the person achieve their problem-related goal. Here is an example from a session which I first introduced at the end of the last principle.

Windy: Apart from feeling guilty about upsetting your sister-in-law what are your options about how to respond to her upset feelings?

Volunteer: Well, I could be indifferent to her upset or I could care but not care too much about her feelings?

Windy: Which would be the healthier goal for you.

Volunteer: To care but not too much.

Windy.   What would you call the feeling where you would care about upsetting your sister-in-law, but not care too much?

Volunteer: Feeling regretful.

Windy: So, if you felt regretful and not guilty about upsetting her feelings, what impact would that have on your behaviour?

Volunteer: I would say no to her request for me to babysit when it was inconvenient for me.

Windy: So, your choice is to continue to feel guilty about upsetting your sister-in-law and not saying 'no' to her when it was in your interests to do so or to feel regretful about upsetting her but saying 'no' when you needed to do so. Which direction would you like to take?

Volunteer: Definitely, the latter.

[*This is the person's problem-related goal.*]

Windy: What would like to achieve on this issue from or conversation today?

Volunteer: I would like to learn the tools to enable me to do this.

[*This is the person's session goal.*]

In my experience, session goals like the one above represent the person's wish to find a solution to their problem which if they were to implement would help them to achieve their problem-related goal. This is shown below:

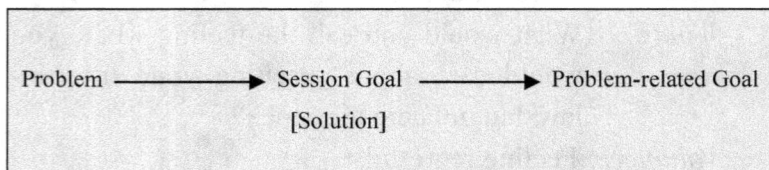

Problem ⟶ Session Goal ⟶ Problem-related Goal
[Solution]

Searching for a Solution

As noted above a solution is something that helps the person address their problem so that they can achieve their problem-related goal. In this section, I will discuss what SST and REBT contributes to my work as I strive to help the person find a good solution to their nominated problem.

Insights from SST

When I reach the part of the live therapy demonstration, when the volunteer and I are searching for a solution to their problem, particularly when I am demonstrating SST, I use the following insights from SST.

PREVIOUS ATTEMPTS TO SOLVE THE PROBLEM

It is especially useful for me to discover what the person has tried in the past to address the problem effectively. To this end I want to discover what they have tried that has proven helpful to them and what they have tried that has proven unhelpful. In discovering this, I encourage the person to build on the former and to set aside the latter as we work towards constructing a solution.

PREVIOUS ATTEMPTS TO SOLVE SIMILAR PROBLEMS

I also ask the person what previous attempts they have made to solve similar problems and suggest that they incorporate the helpful elements of these attempts in the solution of their nominated problem, if relevant and again to set aside the attempts that proved unhelpful.

SUCCESSFUL ATTEMPTS TO SOLVE UNRELATED PROBLEMS

Particularly if my enquiries about the person's previous attempts to solve the same and similar problems have yielded little useful information, I will ask the person to identify successful attempts to solve unrelated problems to see if we can make use of such information in the search for a solution to their nominated problem.

HOW WOULD OTHERS SUCCESSFULLY SOLVE THE PROBLEM?

Another fruitful avenue here is to ask the person to reflect on how others might successfully solve their nominated problem to determine if they can use any of these successful strategies to solve their own problem.

INTERNAL RESOURCES

SST is a strengths-based way of working therapeutically with people. This involves me as a therapist discovering what strengths the person has that they may use in developing and implementing the best solution to their nominated problem. If a person denies that they have any strengths, then I would ask them what people who know them very well would say in response to the same question. Also, I may ask them what they would say if called upon to detail their strengths at an interview for a job they really wanted. Would they really answer that they have no strengths in this context?

There are two types of strengths that I encourage a person to identify: a) tough-minded strengths (e.g. persistence, resilience, and distress tolerance) and b) tender-minded strengths (e.g. acceptance, empathy and kindness). In addition to strengths, I encourage the person to specify the values that they have that may be of most use in helping them to develop and implement a solution to their problem.

VALUES

Russ Harris (2019: 212) argues that 'values are words that describe how we want to behave in this moment and on an ongoing basis. In other words, values are your heart's deepest desires for how you want to behave – how you want to treat yourself, others, and the world around you.' I find that asking the volunteer about their core values at salient points in the live therapy demonstration can help us both in the search for a solution.

EXTERNAL RESOURCES

In addition to the person's internal resources, the volunteer may be encouraged to think of a number of external resources that may be helpful to them as they search for a solution. The following may be useful in this respect (Dryden, 2019b).

- People known to the volunteer who may be useful in some way in helping them solve their problem
- People not known by the volunteer but whom the person might consult for help
- Organisations that may be useful to the volunteer their problem-solving efforts and
- Internet sites that might provide useful problem-solving information.

INSIGHTS FROM A VARIETY OF THERAPEUTIC APPROACHES

When I am doing a live demonstration of SST, then I will use insights from a variety of therapeutic approaches depending on my understanding of the volunteer's nominated problem and how they can best solve it. SST can be practised by therapists who favour a number of different approaches and each therapist will no doubt offer a volunteer solutions suggested by their favoured approach. In the next section I will discuss what REBT has to offer volunteers as they search for a solution to their nominated problem. While I will primarily use these insights in my live demonstrations of REBT, I also use them in my live demonstrations of SST.

Insights from REBT

If I am giving a live demonstration of REBT, I have already helped the volunteer to understand their nominated problem using the ABC framework which

I discussed earlier in their principle. REBT suggests a number of solutions to the volunteer's problem: (i) an attitude change solution; (ii) an inference change solution; (iii) a frame change solution; (iv) a behaviour change solution and (v) an environment change solution.

AN ATTITUDE CHANGE SOLUTION

REBT primarily suggests an attitude change solution to the volunteer's problem and, in particular, one that involves them developing a flexible/non-extreme attitude so that they can respond effectively to the adversity that primarily features in their problem, the existence of which is explained by the rigid/extreme attitude which the person holds towards the adversity. As described in Principle 5, the method that I devised called 'Windy's Review Assessment Procedure' (WRAP) should ideally have helped the volunteer to understand that their problem is based on a rigid/extreme attitude and their goal is based on their alternative flexible/non-extreme attitude. In order to select which attitude to take forward I employ a method that I have devised which I call 'Windy's Choice-based Method of Examining Attitudes'. Here is what I do when using this method.

- I ask the person to focus their rigid attitude and their flexible attitude.[15]
- Then, I ask the person which attitude is true and which is false and to give reasons for their choice.
- Next, I ask them which attitude is logical and which illogical false and to give reasons for their choice.
- Next, I ask them attitude is helpful and which unhelpful and to give reasons for their choice.
- Following on from the above, I ask the person which attitude they would teach their children and to give reasons for their choice.
- Then, I ask them to which attitude they wish to commit themself going forward and to give reasons for their choice.
- Finally, I ask the person to voice any doubts, reservations they have about their decision and I deal with their responses

Assuming that they have chosen their flexible/non-extreme attitude, they are ready to implement this, which I will do later in this principle.

There are instances, particularly in live demonstrations of REBT, where the person is not interested in or does not find value in the attitude

---

[15] These instructions can also be used when asking the person to examine any extreme/non-extreme attitude pairing.

change solution. As described above, when this happens, REBT suggests the use of other solutions.

AN INFERENCE CHANGE SOLUTION

This involves helping the person to examine the inference that constitutes their adversity so that it is no longer an adversity. An example might be a volunteer who has a problem with hurt feelings because they infer that their friend has rejected them. Here we would look at the evidence for and against this inference of 'rejection' and to see if a different, less pejorative inferences accounts for the data (e.g. 'my friend was preoccupied with an issue in her life and did not reject me').

A FRAME CHANGE SOLUTION

Also known as 'reframing', this solution puts the person's problem into a totally different frame so that it is not only no longer a problem; rather, it is a positive aspect of the person's life. Helping a volunteer to see that what they deem to be a problem with hurt, for instance, is in fact evidence of how much the person cares would be an example of this type of change.

A BEHAVIOUR CHANGE SOLUTION

Here, the person solves their problem by changing their behaviour without initially changing their attitude or adversity-based inference. Later attitude change may result from such behaviour change, particularly when the outcome of the behaviour change is positive. An example here is the person who resolves to assert herself with a friend who she thinks has unfairly criticised her and with whom she is angry.

AN ENVIRONMENT CHANGE SOLUTION

Here, the person decides to change the environment in which they experience their problem. An example would be a volunteer who is angry towards her boss for taking advantage of her decides in the session to leave her job and look for another one with a more pleasant boss.

Rehearsing the Solution

Once a person has selected a solution then, where practicable, it is helpful to give them an opportunity to rehearse the solution in the session. Such rehearsal gives the person the experience of what it is like to implement the solution and helps them determine whether or not they think they can make the solution work. It also gives us both an indication of any aspect of the solution that needs to be modified based on the person's experience of rehearsing it and on my observation of that rehearsal.

Forms of Practice
The volunteer can practise the solution in the session in several ways.

MENTAL REHEARSAL
Mental rehearsal involves the person picturing themself implementing the solution in their mind's eye.

Mental rehearsal of a behavioural solution: When the volunteer imagines themself putting their chosen behavioural solution into practice, it is best if they do so realistically rather than perfectly as a perfect performance is unlikely to occur in real life and failure to live up to the ideal standard may discourage the person from persisting with the behavioural solution.

If the person struggles to picture themself implementing their behavioural solution, they can be encouraged to imagine a role model doing so, again realistically and not perfectly. Then they can imitate the role model but in their own style.

Rehearsing the attitudinal solution *(particularly in REBT):* I discussed earlier that REBT favours an attitude change solution to the person's nominated problem. Once such a solution has been selected by the person, I will encourage them to rehearse it. This may involve them engaging a) in a dialogue between a part of themself holding a rigid/extreme attitude and another holding the alternative flexible/non-extreme attitude or b) in a role play where I hold the former attitude and they hold the latter one.

Mental rehearsal of cognitive-behavioural solution: When the person can imagine themself acting constructively while holding a chosen healthy mindset, then this combination is particularly powerful in facilitating change. In REBT, I will discuss the importance of behaviourally implementing the selected attitude in the next section of this principle.

BEHAVIOURAL REHEARSAL

Behavioural rehearsal involves the person practising the behavioural solution in the session. When this involves the volunteer acting in a different way towards another person, the person can do so while imaging the presence of the other or I might play the role of the other.

As noted above, doing this can enable both the volunteer and myself to reflect on the person's behaviour and make appropriate modifications which are then incorporated in a reprise of the behavioural rehearsal. Working in this way, the person ends up with a clearer, more refined form of the behavioural solution.

As with mental rehearsal of a cognitive-behavioural solution (see above), when the person is practising this solution in the session, I first encourage them to get into the appropriate mindset before they rehearse the requisite behaviour and to maintain the mindset throughout the practice of the solution.

CHAIRWORK

Chairwork involves the person addressing their problem while using chairs to facilitate dialogue between self and others or between different parts of self. As such, chairwork gives the person an opportunity to rehearse their chosen solution where it involves such dialogue. This is challenging to do online although Pugh, Bell & Dixon (in press) have argued that it can still be done with appropriate modification.

Planning to Implement the Solution

One of the purposes of rehearsing the solution for the volunteer is for the person to confirm that they wish to implement the solution going forward. Once they do this, I will encourage the person to plan to do so. Implementation involves me helping the person to specify what they are going to do, where they are going to it and how frequently. For me, two important issues are: (i) that the person implements their selected solution while facing the adversity that features in their problem and (ii) that the person can integrate the solution into their life. If they cannot do the latter, then they will not implement the solution consistently.

Helping the Volunteer to Implement the Attitudinal Solution

While rehearsing the attitudinal choice involves the volunteer practising the cognitive features of this attitude in the session, implementing this solution involves the person taking action in ways that are consistent with the chosen attitude and which serves to strengthen the person's conviction it.[16] The greater conviction the person has in their selected attitudinal solution, the more likely it is that this solution will help the person achieve their problem-related goal in due course.

Helping the Volunteer to Identify and Deal with Obstacles to Solution Implementation

After agreeing a solution implementation plan with the volunteer and if there is time, I find it useful to ask the person if they foresee any obstacles to them putting the plan into practice. If so, I encourage them to think of ways of preventing an obstacle from

---

[16] This is particularly the case in my live demonstrations of REBT but also in some cases in my live demonstrations of single-session therapy.

happening or how they can effectively address if it does occur.

*

In this principle I have considered various issues with respect to facilitating change in the live therapy demonstration. In particular, I discussed the importance of working with the volunteer's goals, issues that need to be considered when helping the person to search for a solution, having the person rehearse the solution once one has been selected and working with them to devise a plan to implement the solution.

In the final principle, I will discuss how to end the live therapy demonstration and the answering questions from the audience after the session has come to an end.

PRINCIPLE 7

Ending Live Therapy Demonstrations on a Good Note and What Follows

Introduction

In this final principle, I will stress the importance of ending live therapy demonstrations on a good note. When the volunteer and I have discussed them implementing the agreed solution, this tells me that the session is coming to an end. As such I have several tasks to achieve, depending on the time at my disposal. These include encouraging the volunteer to summarise what we have covered and what they are going to take away from the session, dealing with any unfinished business and discussing, if relevant how the person can generalise their learning to other problems that they may have. Then, I will discuss the role of the audience in the process and finally I will explain why I routinely record my live therapy demonstrations and have them transcribed and how these resources are used.

Asking for the Person's Summary of the Session

Part of ending the live therapy demonstration involves me asking the volunteer to provide a summary of what we covered in the session. I could, of course, provide a summary myself, but I am more interested in the person's summary since that will have more influence of what they will take away from the session than my summary will. Once the person has provided their summary, I might add one or two salient points that the person omitted if I think that it is important to do so.

I sometimes ask a volunteer earlier on in the session to summarise where we have got to so far as a way of punctuating the work we have done and to give them the opportunity to take the session forward based on their summary. However, the final summary is linked more closely to what the volunteer is going to take away from the session.

Focusing on the Person's Takeaway

What the volunteer takes away from the session should ideally be the solution and how to implement it. If the person mentions anything else, I will help them see the connection between that and the solution. Sometimes it is useful for the person to make a note of the takeaway although as I will mention presently, the recording and transcript of the session is available to the volunteer on request and such information can be taken from these resources.

Dealing with Unfinished Business

Ending a live demonstration session well depends on the volunteer leaving the session having told me everything they needed to tell me with respect to their nominated problem and having asked everything they wanted to ask me. To that end, I will invite the volunteer to do both before ending the session, assuming there is sufficient time available to do so. It is important that this invitation is restricted to the person's nominated problem because otherwise they might begin to tell me about a different issue which will muddy the waters should I respond to this newly raised concern.

Prompting Generalisation

If there is time and the work that I have done with the volunteer warrants me doing so, then I will raise the issue concerning how they might generalise their takeaway to other problems that they might have. For example, if a person's takeaway from a live therapy demonstration has been that they do not have to let their boss's presumed negative definition of them become their own definition of themself, I will ask them whether they can apply this takeaway to other problematic situations. If so, I will suggest that they reflect on this point later and develop a plan of action to implement this learning in the same way as we did with their nominated problem during the session. It is important to remember, however, that as time is limited in a live therapy demonstration, such generalisation work can only be minimal.

The Role of the Audience

Once the live therapy demonstration has ended, then I generally turn to the audience members to give them an opportunity to comment on or ask questions about the session that we have just completed. These questions will be directed to myself, to the volunteer and sometimes to both of us. If the audience are physically present in the room (as they would have been pre-pandemic), then I will serve as the moderator calling upon audience members who have their hand raised to speak. If the audience is online, then generally somebody else (usually the workshop organiser) serves as the moderator. The moderator may do one of two things. First, they may call upon an audience member to 'unmute' themself[17] and ask their own question or make their own comment. Second, they may read the question or comment that has been written in the chatbox of the online platform being used.

Given that the live therapy demonstrations that I do are largely (but not exclusively) done in the context of professional training workshops and the like, the comments made, and questions asked reflect this fact.

Comments and Questions to the Volunteer

Almost exclusively, comments made to the volunteer are supportive and complimentary with many people saying how brave they consider the person to be for volunteering and discussing their problem in front of the audience. Perhaps the most common question directed to the volunteer concerns how they felt during the session. Additionally, because I do ask a lot of questions while conducting a live therapy demonstration, the volunteer is often asked how it felt to be asked such questions. Sometimes, audience

---

[17] The pandemic has meant an exponential rise in the use of online platforms for training workshops in counselling and psychotherapy. This has given rise to terms rarely heard in pre-pandemic times. Thus, to 'unmute' oneself means clicking a small red microphone, on 'Zoom' for example, ensuring that the person can now speak and be heard by all members of the audience. Members are generally muted during live therapy demonstrations that are done online to prevent their voices and other sounds being heard by the volunteer and myself, which would be highly disruptive.

members ask the person more about their problem, a practice that I discourage because it tends to re-open a therapeutic discussion that I already have concluded.

Comments and Questions Directed to Me

The comments and questions that I get from audience members depend on the type of demonstration session that I am conducting and the nature of the audience. If I am doing a live demonstration of single-session therapy, that audience is likely to be mixed in the therapeutic approaches that they favour. When commenting on live SST demonstrations, audience members sometimes put forward a different perspective on the problem than I took during the session. When this happens, I suggest that the volunteer gives this perspective serious thought and if I can see a way of blending these two different perspectives, then I will do so. For example, when an audience member suggests a psychodynamic explanation of the problem, I state that this explanation may be correct, but even if it is, the volunteer still has to address the attitudes and behaviours that explain the present existence of their nominated problem.

If I am doing a live demonstration of REBT, then the audience members tend to be primarily interested in REBT and ask me questions about the session that relate to REBT theory and practice.

Sometimes, audience members may suggest how they would have taken a different tack and sometimes their suggestions have validity. If not, I will be respectful, but explain clearly why I think that the audience member is incorrect.

As I pointed out in Principle 1, the two major purposes of live therapy demonstrations are to educate the professional audience and to promote the well-being of volunteers and I will keep these points in mind during the Q&A period. Thus, if a member of the audience suggests something that I consider to be potentially harmful to the well-being of the volunteer again I will show the audience member respect, but I will clearly explain why I think that the suggestion is problematic.

Making the Recording and Transcript of the Live Demonstrations Session Available to the Volunteer

One of the features of my approach to live therapy demonstrations is that I will, with the volunteer's permission, make a digital voice recording of the session which I will later have transcribed by a professional transcriber. I will send both to the volunteer on request. These both aid the volunteer's reflection process after the session and serve to remind the person of what they have learned in the session. Sometimes, these resources enable the person to focus on aspects of the session that seem more important on review than they did at the time. In particular, both resources provide accurate references to the summary that the volunteer person has made at the end of the session as well as what their takeaway has been from the session.

Given the vagaries of the human memory, both the recording and the transcript provide an accurate reminder of what was covered in the live therapy demonstration session and are valuable in this respect. Different volunteers value these media differently. Some value both, while others value one over the other, partly dependent on their learning style. Volunteers who find the written word more helpful will value the transcript while others who learn better by listening will listen to the recording on an mp3 player, smartphone or tablet. People who don't like listening to the sound of their own voice definitely prefer the transcript. It is for these reasons that I provide them with both the recording and the transcript (see Dryden, 2017).

I also use the recording and transcript for my own professional development. Thus, I will review both with the purpose of determining how I might improve my practice in conducting live therapy demonstrations. To this end, I will now present written transcripts of one live demonstration of SST and one live demonstration of REBT to demonstrate my practice of both. My accompanying commentary will demonstrate, in part, how I learn from my own practice. However, the main purpose of including these demonstration sessions in this book is to show how and to what extend I practise what I preach.

*

In this final principle, I have discussed issues that need to be borne in mind when bringing a live therapy demonstration session to a satisfactory conclusion. I then explored the role of the audience in the period directly after the session has finished and I brought the principle to an end by commenting on my use of the digital voice recordings and transcripts that I make of these demonstrations. I will now present examples of my live therapy demonstrations of both SST (Appendix 1) and REBT (Appendix 2). I hope that these transcripts will serve as a suitable conclusion to this book.

If you would care to give me feedback on this book, I would be pleased to receive it at windy@windydryden.com

APPENDIX 1

A Live Demonstration of Single-Session Therapy with Commentary

I did this live demonstration session at a one-day online workshop on 'Single-Session Therapy' on 25/03/21. It lasted 28 minutes 54 secs.

Windy: Hi Jane, what's your understanding of the purpose of our conversation this afternoon?

Jane: To help me understand my reaction to the situation and how I could improve my reaction in future.

Windy: OK. So, it's based on, first of all, understanding how you react to the situation with the possibility of improving it?

Jane: Well, if I'm at fault, yeah.

Windy: If you're at fault or if it's down to you to change.

Jane: Yeah.

Windy: OK. Would you like to tell me a little bit more about the issue?

Jane: Usually I work two days a week in palliative care as a clinical nurse specialist and I've been there for 20 years now and I'm usually the calm

111

one in the team. And I had a ruptured disc back in November. And I was quite happy in my role in the community, really happy, actually, in my work there before I went off with my ruptured disc. And, when I came back on a phased return, my manager told me that I was to stay in the hospital and do my mandatory training, which we have an awful lot of mandatory training to do and it had fallen behind with me being off sick, which I quite understood, going back on a phased return and just being in one day a week for a few weeks, then two days a week and using up some holiday. So, I was quite happy to actually do that.

Then I asked her when I would be going back in the community and she just kept avoiding the question and she just kept saying, 'You need to do this mandatory training and you'll be staying in the hospital until you've done your mandatory training.' I don't usually get anxious, but it just made me feel incredibly anxious, I think the thought that I might be losing my community post, because I've worked in the community for 20 years and we do also cover the hospital setting as well, which I hate and she knows that I hate the hospital setting. So, I put myself into check and said to myself, 'This is only a phased return. Just take a day at a time.'

So, when I next saw her, because she had holiday, she was off, so, when I next saw her, I asked her when I would be returning to the community. So, she then said to me that she was keeping me in the hospital, that she wanted to look after me, that after my back injury she didn't want me getting in and out of a car and she wanted me to stay in the hospital. But what she failed to realise was that I know that she has mismanaged the staffing levels in the hospital. She upset somebody by putting them in the hospital and they left, which left the hospital team very short-staffed and other colleagues have actually been doing extra days to cover for quite a number of months.

So, I then had another conversation with her after her conversation telling me that she was doing it to help my back. I then went to her the next day and said...

Windy: Sorry, that was the second conversation you had with her?

Jane: Yeah.

Windy: And she reiterated that she was doing it because she was trying to protect you because of your back?

Jane: Yeah. So, then I had a third conversation with her the following day and said to her that I felt that she was being evasive about what I was asking her and that the problem really, it wasn't my back that was the issue, it was the fact that she wanted the hospital covered. And I said, 'I don't mind covering the hospital if I'm asked'; that I'd worked in the health service for many years and I'd always been asked. But she just avoided the question of being asked and she just said, 'I want you to help us out,' and that was how it was left, really.

Windy: OK. So, you don't mind doing the work so much – although you'd much prefer to be in the community – if she had come to you, been honest I would imagine, and then ask you if you could help her out.

Jane: Yeah, absolutely. If she'd had the decency to have said to me in the first place, 'You're back on your phased return to work. We're short in the hospital. Would you mind?' then I would've said, 'Well, as you know, I do not like the hospital,' but then I would've considered admitting that I would help her out for two weeks or four weeks.

Windy: Right. So, if she had been open and clear, you would be prepared to help out for a limited period of time between two and four weeks.

Jane: Yeah, but she'd put me in a place that I'm not usually in and, as much as I tried to control my anxiety,… it was very difficult and I felt almost a grievance against her. Obviously, I wouldn't take up the grievance because that would make it worse for both of us.

Windy: So, what place did she put you in?

Jane: She put me in a place where an anxiety about covering the wards, and I think the fact that she didn't ask me made me feel disrespected.

Windy: OK. It's useful if I can ask you some questions just to be clear about some of the factors involved. Is that OK with you?

[It seemed important for Jane to tell me the context to her problem. I was happy to listen and convey my understanding. I seek permission to ask her some questions which will help me to create a focus with her.]

Jane: Yeah, of course.

Windy: OK. So, if she had asked you within the context of her situation – that she needed you to help out – would you have been anxious about working on the ward?

Jane: I would've still been anxious, yeah.

Windy: You would've still been anxious. So, whether or not she'd asked you, you would've still been anxious.

Jane: I think the fact that she wasn't giving me enough information when I first came back, she wasn't laying her cards on the table, so to speak.

Windy: Right, and how did you feel about her being evasive and not putting her cards on the table? You mentioned that she was disrespecting you. Is that what you meant by being evasive and not putting her cards on the table, that she was disrespecting you?

Jane: Yeah, she wasn't giving me the right information. She was telling me that I was to stay in the hospital until I'd done my mandatory training.

Windy: Right. So, how would you put it? She was?

Jane: She wasn't giving me a choice, whereas I would always do my mandatory training even if I was in the community; I would block off half the day, which she knows, to do that training. She was almost, not a bully, but..., yeah, she was... making me feel uncomfortable.

Windy: And how did you feel about her behaviour which may have been separate from the anxiety about going back to work on the ward? How would you describe your feelings about how she treated you?

Jane: I felt resentful to her, probably.

Windy: Yeah, OK. So, you felt resentful about the way she treated you and you felt anxious about going back to the ward, which you would've felt anyway whether you'd go back in order to help out or that you'd go back under the circumstances where you feel you don't have any choice.

Jane: Yeah.

Windy: So, have I understood the situation from your perspective there?

Jane: Yeah. Well, normally on the wards there would've been at least two clinical nurse specialists on the ward at each time, but, because of her staffing levels, there would've only been one of us, and the hospital can be an extremely busy place: you don't know how many people you might have to see; it's unpredictable.

Windy: Right, OK. So, what aspect of this would you like to focus on with the respect of understanding it and perhaps improving it? Your anxiety or your resentment?

[My questions have helped me to see that Jane is struggling with two problems: anxiety and resentment. I ask her on which one of the tow problems would she like to.]

Jane: ... Well, it's kind of a bit of both, but I think I've dealt with the anxiety and I've dealt with the resentment to a certain extent, because I've got to work with her. ... But... could I have dealt with it better myself? I'm not sure.

[Note that Jane selects neither issue because she has dealt with them to some extent.]

Windy: OK. So, that's the question that you're asking yourself now, if I understand you correctly: looking back at the way you dealt with it, could you have dealt with it better?

Jane: Yeah, or was I justified? I felt I was justified in feeling disrespected and not well-informed. … But she wouldn't acknowledge that, you see.

Windy: OK. For me – and I don't know how you feel – being disrespected is not a feeling necessarily but it's a way of thinking about the way somebody has treated you: they've either treated you in a disrespected manner or not, OK?

Jane: Yeah.

Windy: Does that make sense?

Jane: Yeah.

Windy: And then you have feelings of resentment about being disrespected?

Jane: Yeah.

Windy: So, the question is on that point, 'Have I been disrespected or not?' When you say, 'Was I justified?' could you just say a little bit more about that? 'Was I justified,' in what?
              [I am not sure what Jane means here so I ask her to clarify what she meant by 'was I justified'?]

Jane: Well, that's how I felt: that… I wasn't respected.

Windy: OK.

Jane: I would've done things differently. If I'd have been a manager, and I have been a manager, I wouldn't have let a colleague come back without them being fully informed.

Windy: And would you have regarded that to be a respectful way in dealing with that colleague?

Jane: Yeah, to keep them fully informed.

Windy: Right. So, part of being treated respectfully as a manager is to keep the person who you're managing fully informed.

Jane: Yeah, and also, if I was the manager, if they had got anxieties about moving to an area that they weren't comfortable with, it's about listening to those anxieties, in my mind, and supporting that person in that role.

Windy: Right. So, listening to them and supporting them. Do you regard that as a part of respecting the person or would you say that that was some other quality?

Jane: Yeah, I think it's respecting your colleague, isn't it?

Windy: OK. So, if I could understand this, for you, as a manager, showing respect to somebody that you're managing is to, (1) be transparent, be clear, be open, (2) show understanding if the person has some anxiety about going back, and offering to support them.

Jane: Yeah.

Windy: OK. And you're clear about that? You're clear that that is evidence of respect?

Jane: I think so.

Windy: And are you clear that the opposite is evidence of disrespect, which is not being transparent,

hiding things, not understanding and not
supporting?

Jane: Yeah, and not being listened to.

Windy: And not being listened to. Now, which category
does your manager come into?

Jane: I would say she's disrespectful.

Windy: Right. On the grounds that she?

Jane: She didn't really want to listen, or she listened
but she didn't want to do anything about it. On
my return to work, she didn't give me the full
information of what she intended to do with me.

Windy: Right, OK.

Jane: So, I came back, as I probably would've
normally done after being off sick years ago, to
a phased return and then returning back to my
role in the community.

Windy: I'm with you, yeah. And, if you had a nursing
colleague who was doing a similar job to you,
telling you about her manager, the way her
manager treated her, if she came back after a
phased return and she said to you, 'You know,
Jane, my manager is not being open about the
reason why she wants me to go back, she
doesn't understand how I feel about going back,
she's not supporting me, do you think she's
showing me respect or disrespect?' what would
you say?

Jane: Disrespect.

Windy: OK. And, so, listen, I'm curious about
something. Why are you smiling?

Jane:	No, I'm just wondering what you're curious about.
Windy:	OK, because you said, 'I don't know whether the way I'm responding is,' what was the word you used? Is it justified?
Jane:	Justified, yeah.
Windy:	OK. So, having heard me help you to put it into a couple of different scenarios, what do you think about your own question?
Jane:	Yeah, I think it's justified.

[*My questions in the above part of the conversation were meant to help me clarify Jane's position and create a focus. Note that after this sequence, I then asked her to answer her own question about whether she was justified and, in her response, and she replies that she was.*]

Windy:	Right. Why do you say that?
Jane:	Because, if it was a colleague, I would expect her to have been fully informed and supported if she was able to voice her opinions of her anxieties. I would have expected her manager to be supporting her in her phased return back to work.
Windy:	OK. So, you would've thought that she was justified in her interpretation that she was being treated with disrespect, is that right?
Jane:	Yeah.

Windy: Now, if you put you in there, are you justified in making the same interpretation?

Jane: Yeah.

Windy: Is there a hesitation there?

Jane: No.

Windy: No, OK. So, do you want to summarise the work that we've done so far, Jane?

Jane: … Yeah. … You're helping me to validate my feelings… as to whether I'm justified in feeling that I was disrespected and not supported by my manager.

[As part of Jane's summary, she notes that I am helping her to validate her feelings. This was not the intent of my questions – which were to help me clarify and understand, but from perspective clearly this was the effect.]

Windy: Right. And what's your conclusion about the work that we've done?

Jane: Yeah, I think I wasn't supported by my manager.

Windy: Right. Now, you said at the beginning that you wanted help in understanding your reaction as a prelude to taking action on the basis of that understanding. Is that correct?

[Here I return to Jane's her opening statement that she wants to understand her reaction and take action on the basis of this understanding.]

Jane: Yeah.

Windy: So, have you got the understanding that you were looking for?

Jane: Yeah, I think I've validated that I was justified in feeling that way.

Windy: Who validated it?

Jane: Myself.

Windy: That's right. I was just asking you questions.

Jane: Yeah.

Windy: Now, on the basis of that validation, Jane, how do you plan to go forward with that understanding in terms of any actions that you might be thinking of taking?

Jane: It's a difficult one because I could have a grievance with her, which I could take through the Royal College of Nursing or go to her higher manager, but that wouldn't be acting in her best interest or in my best interests, and she's not a bad person.

Windy: So, you could take a grievance.

Jane: I could take a grievance.

Windy: Or you could go to her manager.

Jane: Yeah, or I could go to her manager, or I could just accept the situation as it is.

Windy: Right. Would you like to hear a fourth option? [*Here, Jane and I are reviewing her behavioural options. We outlined three such options and I ask her if she wants to hear my ideas of a fourth option.*]

Jane: Yeah.

Windy: It's my day for offering options, you realise that?[18] I don't know how well you know this person so that's got to be put in the context of that, but, from what you were saying – that you previously got on reasonably well with her and it's not as if you've got an enduringly bad relationship, is that correct?

Jane: Yeah. I wouldn't say I've been her manager, but I've been higher than her professionally for many years, and then she's come into this role because I encouraged her to come into this role and encouraged her to be in the role that she's in now. So, I encouraged her to be where she is today.

Windy: Sure.

Jane: So, I'm proud of what she's done, really.

Windy: Right, OK. And maybe, in terms of the missing option that I'm going to put to you, you could put the missing option in that context: that you're proud about what she's achieved. Now, my option to put on the table to think about is for you to take her through exactly the same process as I took you.

Jane: Right. ... [*Pause*] That's a good idea.

Windy: What do you think of that?

Jane: ... Yeah.

Windy: Can you imagine yourself doing that?

---

[18] This refers to the previous live therapy demonstration I did.

Jane: She wouldn't like that.

Windy: Well, she's not going to like having a grievance against her, is she?

Jane: No.

Windy: She's not going to like it if you go to her manager.

Jane: No.

Windy: Is there anything that you can do that she is going to like?

Jane: Put up and shut up.

Windy: Well, yeah. Are you prepared to do that?

Jane: … She's actually on holiday this week. I could actually say to her, when she comes back, 'I've been reflecting on this incident that has really upset me,' and I could say to her, 'Can I ask you to put yourself in my shoes?' and give her the information that she gave me.

           [*Jane has indicated that she likes my fourth option and has begun to explore it.*]

Windy: Yeah, and how would she have responded if her manager had treated her in that way.

Jane: Yeah.

Windy: OK.

Jane: She's… quite a stoic character.

Windy: Meaning what?

Jane: She doesn't really give anything of herself away.

Windy: OK.

Jane: And…, yeah, she… [*pause*] kind of puts herself
              as a bit of a tough cookie, if you know what I
              mean?

Windy: Right. So, you might want to suggest that she
              might think about the questions you put to her
              and then come back to you rather than make a
              judgement there and then.

Jane: Yeah.

Windy: Because it sounds like to me that you're faced
              with four options, none of which you're going
              to hold a party about. You don't want to put up
              and shut up, you don't want to take a grievance,
              ideally you'd like her to come to you and say,
              'Yeah, I've been thinking about this on my own
              and I think I've treated you unfairly,' but let's
              assume that that's not an option. It sounds like
              you've got a choice of the lesser of four evils or
              bad things.

              [*Here, I summarise the four options.*]

Jane: Yeah.

Windy: Which one would sit most with your values as a
              person?

              [*In Principle 6, I discussed using values to help
              a person solve a problem and this is the
              approach I adopt at this point.*]

Jane: Speaking to her, not going behind her back and
              not going to her manager.

Windy: Yeah, because I guess, if you were going behind
              her back, in a way it could be construed that

you were doing the same thing as she was doing: not being honest and open.

Jane: Yeah.

Windy: And you wanted her to be honest and open. So, maybe you could be a good role model for her. I don't know.

Jane: Yeah. Well, I gave her three choices; I spoke to her three times. So, yeah, I wouldn't go behind her back.

Windy: OK.

Jane: It's deceitful, isn't it, and it's better to come to an agreement together, isn't it?

Windy: OK. If you can, and it doesn't sound like the 'put up and shut up' is going to change anything.

Jane: No.

Windy: The grievance is just going to put her on high defensive. The going to her manager is going to put her on medium to high defensive, it sounds like.

Jane: Yeah.

Windy: And the option that we're talking about is not great but it's something which you seem to be saying, 'Well, I could do that and I think it might be in accord with my values of being honest and open with her.'

Jane: Yeah, I could do that.

Windy: Do you see any obstacle to doing that, as we think about it, that might stop you from taking her through that particular process in exactly the same way as I took you?

[*Once Jane has selected a solution, I enquire if she foresees any obstacles to her implementing it.*]

Jane: The obstacle would be if she didn't want to listen.

Windy: Right. OK. But then would that be an obstacle that would stop you from doing it or would you do it anyway, knowing that you've actually done your bit which is to put something to her whether she listened or not?

Jane: … [*Pause*] Yeah, I think I'd have to have an attempt to put my case across, wouldn't I?

Windy: Yeah, and I guess one way would be to ask her to see if she's interested in listening to you from beginning to end, rather than to cut off in the middle.

[*I suggest a way around the obstacle here. I do so as we are coming to the end of our conversation.*]

Jane: Yeah.

Windy: Now, again, you don't know whether she's going to do that, but at least you'll be doing your best. So, why don't we summarise where we've got to in terms of the whole picture?

Jane: OK. … [*Pause*] Yeah, I think I've come to terms and validated that I was justified in how I was made to feel by my manager and… come up with a solution to actually go back to her, not to cause any further issues or any further problems, but just to say, 'Can we reflect on what happened to me on my phased return to work and my three conversations with you and how that made me feel? Can I just reflect that back to you?' but... – no, I don't want to do that, do I, 'can I reflect that back to you', but, 'Can I ask you to put yourself in my shoes: that you're coming back from phased return, you've been doing something for 20 years and you're not given the correct information when you return back to work, how would that make you feel?'

[*My request to Jane to summarise the work we have done also serves as a rehearsal of the solution to see how it feels. Note that Jane and I add a few 'tweaks' to the solution stated above, but nothing that substantially changes it.*]

Windy: OK. Now, as you hear yourself saying that, how does it feel?

Jane: I think I'd like to say to her, 'I'm doing this from a learning point of view for both of us.'

Windy: OK.

Jane: And that I'm not being... [long pause] – I can't think of the word I'm trying to say. I'm not... questioning her managerial roles on a whole, but I'm just questioning this one incident that happened.

Windy: OK.

Jane: And I wouldn't want somebody else to feel the way I did on a phased return.

Windy: Yeah, and maybe that you wouldn't want her to feel the way that you did if she was in your situation.

Jane: Exactly, yeah.

Windy: OK. So, have you got what you wanted from today?

Jane: Yes, thank you. Yeah.

Windy: OK, good. Let's get their comments.

APPENDIX 2

A Live Demonstration of Rational Emotive Behaviour Therapy with Commentary

I did this live demonstration session at a weekly one-hour REBT Facebook Group webinar that I give entitled 'Windy Dryden Live!' It took place on 10/05/21 and lasted 17 minutes 15 secs.

Windy: OK, Nina, what's your understanding of the purpose of our conversation today?

Nina: Well, to have an REBT session with yourself and to bring an issue that I wanted to have some help with.

Windy: So, what's the issue you want to be helped with?

Nina: The issue is, this is something I've only really noticed in the last maybe couple of years, two years, and I think it has been holding me back, but I have a real sense of imposter syndrome.

Windy: Hold you back in what area?

[*This question is designed to help Nina select a context for her problem with 'imposter syndrome'.*]

131

Nina: Progressing, really, through work. I feel it's holding me back.

Windy: What's your work?

Nina: Well, I work as a therapist, so a counsellor but also as an independent sexual violence adviser.

Windy: And where do you experience this imposter syndrome?

Nina: Mainly at work rather than in day-to-day life.

Windy: Yeah, but which area of your work? The counselling work or the other work?

Nina: Sometimes both. I have a lot of self-doubt and it crosses over into both.

Windy: OK. Why don't you choose one of those arenas for us to investigate. Which one would you choose?

Nina: OK, I'll go for the ISVA role the Independent Sexual Violence Adviser role.

[I have helped Nina to nominate one the two areas of the work that she experienced her problem.]

Windy: OK. ISVA could also stand for Imposter Syndrome. So, how are you defining imposter syndrome? What do you mean by that?

[When a volunteer uses a concept such as 'imposter syndrome' I ask them to define it.]

Nina: Kind of a feeling that people see me in one way that maybe I don't feel that way myself. So, they might see me as capable, competent, organised, good at my job, and actually a lot of self-doubt creeps in about that.

Windy: Give me a specific example of how this plays out so we can examine it in a little bit more detail?
              [*Note that I am gradually encouraging Nina to be more specific.*]

Nina: How does it play out? ... I suppose supporting a client and maybe... other people just assuming that I'm doing this amazing job and, actually, not necessarily feeling I am myself.

Windy: So, in a situation, how do you know that they think you're doing an amazing job?

Nina: Because they see the positive feedback from clients. ... I suppose I know the role, at the end of the day; I know what I'm doing.

Windy: OK. So, who are these other people, by the way?

Nina: Namely the CEO of the organisation.

Windy: OK. So, the CEO in your organisation sees the clients' feedback and thinks that you're doing a really great job, but you don't necessarily share that view. What kind of view do you have of the job that you're doing?

Nina: I might feel that I haven't done as much perhaps as I could, that I'm duping my CEO into believing that I'm better than perhaps I feel I am.

Windy: Well, OK, so, this idea of you duping the person, you mean what are you doing to dupe the person, because it sounds like, the way you've described it, they don't know what goes on in the counselling room, they're not party to the process, all they see is what the clients say about the process. So, they read the idea that the clients say, 'Oh, this is great,' and they say, 'Nina's doing a really great job,' but, in the therapy room or whatever it is where you work with your clients in this sphere of your activity, you can see, 'Wait a minute, I could've done that better, I could've done that better.' Let's assume that. Let's suppose that you notice that you could do a better job than you're currently doing. When you identify that, how do you feel about that observation?

Nina: ... I suppose I feel a little bit anxious.

Windy: Anxious about what?

Nina: That that might come to light that I haven't done everything I could.

Windy: Because you start off with the idea that you want other people, like your CEO, to know that, not only the clients think you're wonderful but that they don't see that there are certain things that you can do better. So, your preference is for them to not see some of the things that you aren't doing as well as you could, right?

[*In a live demonstration of REBT, I am looking at the outset to find the adversity which here is the CEO and others see that there are things Nina could do better. Then I will show the person that she holds a preference towards the adversity.*]

Nina: Yeah, correct.

Windy: Right, that's fine. But then, when you are anxious and having imposter syndrome, do you think your attitude is, 'I don't want them to see areas where I could improve and, therefore, they must not see that. They must see me as the clients see me,' or are you saying, 'It would be nice if they saw me as clients do and that my performance couldn't be improved upon, but they don't have to see that. They are able to see me warts and all'? Now, when you're anxious, which attitude do you have?

[Here I am using elements of Windy's Review Assessment Procedure (WRAP) to help Nina identify the attitude that underpinned her anxiety-related imposter syndrome and which attitude might constitute the solution to this problem. See Principle 5 for a full description of this procedure.]

Nina: Definitely the first one. So, they must.

Windy: Right.

Nina: Yeah, they must not see the flaws.

Windy: If you really had the second, how would you feel?

Nina: Yeah, it would be nice to feel accepted regardless of the warts and all.

Windy: Yeah, and also don't forget that you can accept you warts and all, because I'm hearing two things there. One is you are really saying, 'Oh my God, they mustn't see that I have these warts. My clients haven't seen it and therefore they mustn't see it and, if they saw it, then that would be terrible.' The other is how do you feel about your own warts when you see it?

Nina: I don't like it very much. It sits uncomfortably with me.

Windy: Right, but how do you feel about seeing your own warts?

Nina: … [*Pause*] How do I feel?

Windy: Yeah.

Nina: Yeah. … Well, I can acknowledge that I'm only human at the end of the day, so I am going to have warts.

Windy: Yeah, but if you really believed that, we wouldn't be having this discussion, would we?

Nina: No. I suppose I'd feel a bit annoyed, really, at myself.

Windy: Because what are you demanding of yourself?

Nina: Demanding that I'm perfect.

Windy: 'I must be wart-free. My clients must love me, my CEO must think I'm great and I must be wart-free for myself and show my CEO that I'm wart-free. If I don't do these things, I'm an imposter.'

[*Given the limited time I have with Nina I use her specific example and show her the more general rigid/extreme attitude that drives her imposter syndrome.*]

Nina: Exactly.

Windy: Well, in which case we all are imposters, because how the hell are we going to live up to that picture of ourselves? The only reason that you have the imposter syndrome is not because of the gap between your performance and how you want to be seen, but because of your attitude towards that gap, and you're demanding that your clients must love you, the CEO must love you and you must be wart-free. That's your imposter syndrome.

Nina: It is, yeah.

Windy: But, if you really showed yourself, 1) 'It would be nice if my clients loved me, but they don't always have to. It would be nice if my CEO didn't see the fact that I can improve, but that wouldn't be terrible if she sees that I could improve – actually, once she sees that, she might even pay for me to go on training courses,' because why the hell should she send you on training courses if you're wart-free, if you're perfect? 'And then I would like to be wart-free,' which is fair enough, 'but I don't have to be. I'm a fallible human being, warts and all.' If you worked on believing that, where would your imposter syndrome be?

[Having outlined the general rigid/extreme attitude that explains her imposter syndrome, I outline the general attitudinal solution to this problem.]

Nina: Well, I suppose it wouldn't really exist anymore.

Windy: That's right, because you would have what we call the 'Nina Syndrome'. Do you know what the Nina Syndrome is?

Nina: My own.

Windy: Yeah, what is it?

Nina: It is that, actually, I would prefer things to be a certain way, but I can accept it if they're not.

Windy: Yeah, 'And I am a person who is going to continue to try to improve as a therapist and a worker, but I am going to make mistakes along the way and I'd better accept myself along that journey.' That's the Nina Syndrome.

[I call the healthy alternative to imposter syndrome 'Nina syndrome' which I hope will be memorable for her.]

Nina: OK.

Windy: So, you have a choice: you could either have the Nina Syndrome or the imposter syndrome.

Nina: Yeah, I think I'd prefer to be my own boss in that situation.

Windy: Fine, OK. Now, are there any doubts that you have about doing that going forward?

Nina: … [*Pause*] No. I was going to say 'losing my job', but actually I don't think it would come to that.

Windy: Yes, that's right. You see, that's the fear. Part of the imposter syndrome is this idea that, 'Unless I show people that I'm perfect, even though I'm not and there's a gap between that, then they'll sack me.' Now, let's have a look at that from an objective point of view. How long have you been working in this organisation?

[Technically, the thought that she will lose her job if people see her imperfections is a thinking consequence of her rigid/extreme attitude. As such it is a distorted inference which I encourage Nina to stand back and examine.]

Nina: I've had a couple of different roles, so probably about eight years now.

Windy: So, you've been working in the organisation for eight years, how many times does your organisation sack therapeutic workers?

Nina: Only once, I think.

Windy: What for?

Nina: … I think it was something inappropriate.

Windy: Right, yeah, not the fact that they made an error.

Nina: No. They did make an error of judgement, but it was a pretty serious one.

Windy: No, a serious one. I'm making a distinction between the kind of error that they made, which was a sackable offence, and the kinds of errors that you might make in the therapeutic room, the kinds of errors that I might make doing these conversations. I could make errors. Matt might sack me. Oh my God!

So, again, if you look objectively at your organisation, then that's going to help you see that, if you keep making mistakes, they might send you on a training course, but, if you might make a really inappropriate mistake, then it's a sackable thing.

Nina: Yeah, definitely.

Windy: So, I'm making a distinction between reading it in a newspaper: if they read what that person in a newspaper, would people say, 'Why did they sack that person?' or would they say, 'I can understand why they sacked that person'?

Nina: Oh yeah, they'd probably say, 'Well, that's really inappropriate.'

Windy: Right. And, if they read in the newspaper that you might have done something wrong – might have asked a question wrong or did something – would they say, 'Yes, they were right to sack her,' or would they say, 'My God, why did they sack this person for that?'?

Nina: They'd probably say, 'That's a bit harsh.'

Windy: Yeah. So, when you have the rigid attitudes that characterise the imposter syndrome, you create an environment which is really harsh. But, when you operate according to the Nina syndrome and the idea you keep all your attitudes flexible, you wouldn't invent that; you'll see the organisation more clearly according to what it is.

Nina: Yeah, definitely, and they are very supportive.

Windy: Yeah, that's right.

Nina: Which is why it seems crazy that I've had this imposter syndrome going on.

Windy: But can you see that you're bound to have the imposter syndrome going on as long as you have the rigid attitudes going on, because the imposter syndrome is based on rigid attitudes. It's based on the idea that, 'Other people see me as competent externally, but I don't feel competent internally because I make mistakes, which I must not make.' That's the root of the imposter syndrome. Is there anything else you want to bring up on this subject?

[*Again, I help Nina to see the relationship between her rigid/extreme attitudes and her imposter syndrome and that these attitudes lead her to create what I referred to as a harsh environment. Once she operates according to what I call Nina syndrome she sees her organisation the way it is.*]

Nina: No. I suspect it goes back to my relationship with my mum.

Windy: Why?

Nina: Not being allowed to make mistakes.

Windy: Why bring your dear old mum into it? What did she do?

Nina: Just about not being able to make mistakes, really.

Windy: No, you were able to make mistakes, let's face it like that, but, in other words, how did your mum respond to your mistakes?

Nina: Oh OK. With a lot of disapproval and freezing out.

Windy: And what did you conclude from that, growing up?

Nina: Well, that it wasn't a good thing to do.

Windy: 'And, if I make these mistakes, what does that prove about me?'?

Nina: I've failed.

Windy: 'And, if I fail, what does that make me, in my mother's eyes?'?

Nina: I'm not lovable.

Windy: 'And what does that make me in my eyes?'?

Nina: Unlovable.

Windy: That's right. I know this is a tall order, but, if you were to have said to yourself about your mother, 'My mother's got some really strange ideas about me. She's demanding that I mustn't make mistakes. How strange that a human being says that about another human being, especially about their daughter. My mother is full of shit. I'm not going to listen to her that much. I'm going to listen to me and my more flexible attitude,' what do you think would've happened if you did that?

Nina: Yeah, life would've been a lot easier.

Windy: That's right.

Nina: I wouldn't be sitting here having this conversation with you.

Windy: That's right. So, it's a combination of what your mother did and what you understandably did, being a younger child, and carried on.

Nina: Yeah.

Windy: Now you have an opportunity to say, 'My mother was wrong and, when I demand perfection, I'm making an error and, although I necessarily can't stop myself from starting that way of thinking, I can really respond to it as quickly as I can. So, I'm not going to try to eliminate it, but I'm going to respond to it when I catch it.'

[*When a person says something like 'it goes back to my relationship with my mum, I respond by saying that (i) the other person was probably operating from their own set of rigid/extreme attitudes; (ii) the volunteer, being much younger, understandably accepted what the other person said uncritically and applied it to themself; (iii) if they had not done so they probably would not have the problem and (iv) they have the opportunity now to change their rigid/extreme attitudes and develop*

> *flexible/non-extreme attitudes which will help them solve their problem now.*]

Nina: Yeah. Great.

Windy: Right. Let's see what the group's got to say.

Nina: Thank you very much, by the way.

Windy: My pleasure.

References

Barber, J. (1990). Miracle cures? Therapeutic consequences of clinical demonstrations. In J. K. Zeig & S. G. Gilligan (eds), *Brief Therapy: Myths, Methods and Metaphors* (pp. 437–42). New York: Brunner-Mazel.

Bloom, B. L. (1981). Focused single-session therapy: Initial development and evaluation. In S. Budman (ed.), *Forms of Brief Therapy* (pp. 167–216). New York: Guilford Press.

Bordin, E. S. (1979). The generalizability of the psychoanalytic concept of the working alliance. *Psychotherapy: Theory, Research and Practice,* 16(3), 252–60.

Constantino, M. J., Glass, C. R., Arnkoff, D. B., Ametrano, R. M., & Smith, J. Z. (2011). Expectations. In J. C. Norcross (ed.*), Psychotherapy Relationship that Work: Evidence-Based Responsiveness. 2nd edition* (pp. 354–76). New York: Oxford University Press.

Cooper, M., & Law, D. (eds). (2018). *Working with Goals in Psychotherapy and Counselling.* Oxford: Oxford University Press.

Dryden, W. (2006). *Counselling in a Nutshell.* London: Sage.

Dryden, W. (2009). *How to Think and Intervene like an REBT Therapist.* Hove, East Sussex, East Sussex: Routledge.

Dryden, W. (2011). *Counselling in a Nutshell. 2nd edition.* London: Sage.

Dryden, W. (2017). *Single-Session Integrated CBT (SSI-CBT): Distinctive Features.* Abingdon, Oxon: Routledge.

Dryden, W. (2018). *Very Brief Therapeutic Conversations.* Abingdon, Oxon: Routledge.

Dryden, W. (2019a). *REBT in India: Very Brief Therapy for Problems of Daily Living.* Abingdon, Oxon: Routledge.

Dryden, W. (2019b). *Single-Session Therapy: 100 Key Points and Techniques.* Abingdon, Oxon: Routledge.

Dryden, W. (2021a). *Seven Principles of Single-Session Therapy.* London: Rationality Publications.

Dryden, W. (2021b). *Seven Principles of Rational Emotive Behaviour Therapy.* London: Rationality Publications.

Dryden, W. (2022). *Understanding Emotional Problems and Their Healthy Alternatives: The REBT Perspective, 2nd Edtion.* Abingdon, Oxon: Routledge.

Ellis, A., & Joffe, D. (2002). A study of volunteer clients who experienced live sessions of rational emotive behavior therapy in front of a public audience. *Journal of Rational-Emotive & Cognitive-Behavior Therapy, 20,* 151–8.

Harris, R. (2019). *ACT Made Simple: An Easy-to-Read Primer on Acceptance and Commitment Primer, 2nd Edtion..* Oakland CA: New Harbinger Publications.

Hopwood, C. J., Swenson, C., Bateman, A., Yeomans, F. E., & Gunderson, J. G. (2014). Approaches to psychotherapy for borderline personality: Demonstrations by four master clinicians. *Personality Disorders: Theory, Research, and Treatment, 5*(1), 108–16.

Hoyt, M. F., Young, J., & Rycroft, P. (2020). Single session thinking 2020. *Australian & New Zealand Journal of Family Therapy,* 41(3), 218–30.

Keller, G., & Papasan, J. (2012). *The One Thing: The Surprisingly Simple Truth behind Extraordinary Results.* Austin, TX: Bard Press.

Lankton, S. R. & Zeig, J. K. (1989). *Extrapolations: Demonstrations of Ericksonian Therapy.* New York: Brunner/Mazel.

Pugh, M., Bell, T., & Dixon, A. (in press). Delivering tele-chairwork: A qualitative survey of expert therapists. Psychotherapy Research.

Rogers, C. R. (1957). The necessary and sufficient conditions of therapeutic personality change.*Journal of Consulting Psychology*, 21, 95–103.

Simon, G. E., Imel, Z. E., Ludman, E. J., & Steinfeld, B. J. (2012). Is dropout after a first psychotherapy visit always a bad outcome? *Psychiatric Services*, 63(7), 705–7.

Talmon, M., Hoyt, M. F., & Rosenbaum, R. (1988). When the first session is the last: A map for rapid therapeutic change. Short course presented to the Third International Congress of Ericksonian Hypnosis and Psychotherapy, San Francisco, December 1988. The Milton H. Erickson Foundation, Phoenix, AZ.

Weinrach, S. G. (2001). Collaborators in the marginalization of REBT: The use and misuse of *Three Approaches to Psychotherapy* and other videotaped demonstrations. *Journal of Rational-Emotive & Cognitive-Behavior Therapy,* 19, 43–54.

Index

149